BREWING REVOLUTION

Brewing Revolution

PIONEERING THE CRAFT BEER MOVEMENT

Frank Appleton

 HARBOUR
PUBLISHING

This book is dedicated to Jean Bassett, and the new generation of Appletons—Andrew, Jodi, Malcolm and Eric.

HARBOUR PUBLISHING CO. LTD.
P.O. Box 219, Madeira Park, BC, VON 2H0
www.harbourpublishing.com

Edited by Arlene Prunkl
Cover illustration by Eduardo Martinez Macias
Text design by Shed Simas
Printed and bound in Canada

Harbour Publishing acknowledges the support of the Canada Council for the Arts, which last year invested $153 million to bring the arts to Canadians throughout the country. We also gratefully acknowledge financial support from the Government of Canada through the Canada Book Fund and from the Province of British Columbia through the BC Arts Council and the Book Publishing Tax Credit.

Canada Council Conseil des arts
for the Arts du Canada

BRITISH COLUMBIA
ARTS COUNCIL
An agency of the Province of British Columbia

Canadä

LIBRARY AND ARCHIVES CANADA CATALOGUING IN PUBLICATION

Appleton, Frank, 1941-, author
    Brewing revolution : pioneering the craft beer movement / Frank Appleton.

Includes bibliographical references.
Issued in print and electronic formats.
ISBN 978-1-55017-782-4 (paperback).--ISBN 978-1-55017-783-1 (html)

    1. Appleton, Frank, 1941-. 2. Brewers--British Columbia--Biography. 3. Microbreweries--Canada--History. 4. Beer industry--Canada--History. I. Title.

TP573.5.A66A3 2016   338.7'6633092   C2016-903674-X
                                                  C2016-903675-8

Contents

Hermit hoar, in solemn cell,
Wearing out life's evening gray;
Strike thy bosom, sage! And tell,
What is bliss, and which the way?
Thus I spoke, and speaking sigh'd,
Scarce repress'd the starting tear,
When the hoary Sage reply'd,
Come, my lad, and drink some beer.

—*Johnsonian Miscellanies*, Samuel Johnson (1709–84)

1 Early Days in Industrial Microbiology

IN 1963 I WAS TWENTY-TWO YEARS OLD AND LIVING IN Manchester, England, where I had been born. I had earned a technical-college diploma in microbiology, gone into the food sciences, taken diploma courses in milk processing and brewing technology and had spent my summers working in a dairy laboratory and a brewery. However, by far the most interesting to me was that I had landed a job developing a small microbiology lab within a huge lab that analyzed the products of a mega factory processing 500 tons of Midwestern United States corn each day into hundreds of different products including glucose, cornstarch and corn oil. The corn was brought in from Chicago 15,000 tons at a time on ocean-going freighters, which navigated the whole St. Lawrence Seaway system and the Atlantic Ocean and came up the Manchester Ship Canal into the heart of the city. Our plant—Brown & Polson—a recent addition to the empire of Corn Products Inc. of Chicago, occupied a fifty-acre site in the industrial area known as Trafford Park, with a dock on the ship canal and huge concrete silos to store the corn.

B&P's corn products went into hundreds of food items but not a single one was for fresh home consumption. In fact, corn (*Zea mays*) was a bit of a mystery to the English. Not native to the country, it was only grown in small amounts on farms for the feeding of pigs and poultry ("chicken corn"). No person I knew had ever tried or even seen fresh corn on the cob, mostly because of the dearth of imported foods in England during and following World War II. I recall buying some canned "sweet corn" from the States in the tiny company store at B&P and taking it home, where my dad and I, with great curiosity, heated it up and served it. Our faces must have been a picture as we tried the slimy, sweet, lumpy mixture. What was it? A vegetable? A fruit? We agreed on one thing—it was awful! And we never tried it again.

Our huge factory operated 24 hours a day in three shifts, with workers numbering in the hundreds and scores of commercial food and drink makers devouring our products by the truckload. By far the most profitable was dextrose (a form of glucose) in liquid and powdered forms. Glucose is a simple sugar used in hundreds of applications such as soft drinks, ice cream and commercial food recipes as well as in a highly purified form by hospitals and even in another form in breweries. At B&P, it was made by "acid hydrolysis," in which a stiff dose of hydrochloric acid was added to a slurry of cornstarch to break the starch down into its components, the simplest one being dextrose. It worked, but in molecular terms it was like putting a charge of dynamite under a house to retrieve the usable building materials: you spend a lot of time clearing debris and throwing stuff out. The process mirrored what happens in the stomach, where the first step in breaking food down to simpler molecules is to subject it to a 3 percent hydrochloric acid environment. However, lacking the enzymes secreted by the body and the microbial flora of the gut, the industrial process was only about 50 percent efficient at turning starch into dextrose, and a huge amount of processing was needed to clean out the other 50 percent of charred starch and sugars.

Then one day somebody in the big laboratory in Chicago, a Scots genius named Angus, said, "There's a better way of doing this, and it's called *Aspergillus oryzae*. It's a mould." He knew about something that had been going on for centuries in Japan: the Japanese made an alcoholic drink called sake from polished white rice that had lost the ability to germinate, and germination is the key to a plant turning its starch into sugars, the first step in making alcohol.

In the process of malting, barley is wetted, just allowed to sprout, then dried. The brewer uses the enzymes created to complete the starch breakdown to sugars, which he can ferment with yeast to produce alcohol. But if you polish off the germ, there will be no germination, no enzymes to break down the starch, no sugars produced and no alcoholic fermentation. So how do the Japanese produce an alcoholic drink from polished rice? They do it by cooking and steam-sterilizing the rice, cooling then infecting it with this mould called *Aspergillus oryzae*, which in growing produced the very amylase enzymes needed to break down the starch. They make a mash of that, strain and cool it, introduce yeast, and in a week or so they have an alcoholic beverage!

Angus reasoned that we could probably do it even better than the sake makers. A big issue, after the rice beds were prepared and infected with *Aspergillus*, was keeping the beds away from light because light caused the fungus to produce spores, which spoiled the taste and appearance. These spores always appeared at the surface of the bed. Angus said, "Why can't we grow it in the dark in a liquid culture that is constantly moving, so the mould has no chance to form a surface layer?" Weren't the starch-splitting enzymes present in the mycelium of the mould, not the spores? Of course they were.

Within a short space of time we had a series of culture flasks bubbling with various starch media and little cotton-ball fluffs of *Aspergillus* dancing around in them. Our analysis showed the mould converted 90 percent of the starch to dextrose compared to 50 percent with the acid hydrolysis process. Case closed. All that was needed was to build a massive plant to produce dextrose by this new method. Meanwhile, we carried out plant trials and cultured batches of *A. oryzae* inoculant in the laboratory and then in a pilot plant. Eventually, 30,000-litre reinforced concrete tanks with epoxy linings became the fermentation tank farm for the process. When these came on-stream and showed that the system worked, the acid hydrolysis plant was phased out. This simple idea, enzyme hydrolysis, had transformed the production of dextrose from cornstarch. The triumph of microbiology!

As an eager student, a few years earlier I had been reading the science writers who were predicting that the new frontier, after the domination of nuclear physics, would be in biology. Penicillin—just the first in a long line of antibiotics for specific purposes—was derived from the *Penicillium* mould. Francis Crick and James Watson had just delineated the DNA molecule and discovered how it replicated itself. The implications of knowing the exact molecular makeup of the stuff that made all plants and animals, including us, was enormous. Enzyme hydrolysis of starch was but a sideshow in the great biology revolution to come, but it was still significant. It proved to me that I was in the right line of work.

I suppose I could have had a fine career with Corn Products Inc., but after the production plant was up and running, the job turned routine: keeping tabs on contaminants, mostly wild yeasts, in the *Aspergillus* fermentations and producing a continuous line of fresh cultures to seed starch slurry batches. No new groundbreaking processing ideas seemed likely to come up, and I began to look for new horizons. To Canada, in fact, a land that had long fascinated me. I had read about the voyageurs, the great explorers David Thompson and Simon Fraser, but especially Grey Owl, the revered Aboriginal sage, conservationist and writer (who turned out to be Archie Belaney, an Englishman). There were lots of great stories to follow up on in this huge land. Besides, I had a sister in Vancouver.

Perhaps it seems strange that, some twenty years after my start with corn products at Brown & Polson, I would be leading the crusade to expunge the widespread use of cornstarch, corn syrup and other non-malt "adjunct" in factory-produced beer in order to return to better, more authentic beers based—as they were historically—on barley malt. But different times make for different thinking.

2 The Dream Job

LIVING IN VANCOUVER IN 1964, I SAW AN AD IN THE paper for a quality control supervisor for an O'Keefe brewery. This plant had been on-stream for just two years and was strategically located for the distribution of its beers at the junction of Lougheed Highway, Boundary Road and the Trans-Canada Highway. It was a showpiece brewery with a beautiful stainless-steel brewhouse proudly displayed in a glass tower above Lougheed Highway. It had lots of space for expansion and nicely maintained gardens around the office block, and inside the main entrance was a conservatory full of plants, with climbing plants surrounding the staircase to the second floor. I had never seen its like in England, where breweries were often more than a hundred years old and definitely not picturesque.

I sent in my resumé and soon after was called for an interview with Gerry Pratt, the brewmaster. Gerry was a friendly, easygoing guy who was impressed with my background, but he pointed out that quality control work was perhaps not as interesting as the cutting-edge work on enzyme hydrolysis of starch using *Aspergillus oryzae* that had been my last job. Nevertheless, after the interview he took me on a tour of the brewery, and we stopped by the office of Harley Deeks, the vice-president and general manager of O'Keefe in Western Canada. Harley was a tall, handsome fellow, full of enthusiasm for his new plant and its staff, and he seemed destined for great things. A microbiology graduate himself, he was interested in the work I had been doing in England.

About a week later I got a call from Gerry saying I had the job. I was overjoyed. True, the work would be pretty routine and somewhat dull—plating out samples of water, beer and yeast in process to detect the presence of invading beer spoilage organisms. However, the plant was kept at an almost hospital level of sanitation; it was unusual for any unwanted bug to show up, unlike the ancient breweries of England, where panic outbreaks of infection of beer in process were common. The plant hummed with enthusiasm for the future: we were launching O'Keefe brands in BC for the first time!

Another great plus for me was that I had a whole new lifestyle. Exchanging grimy, industrial Manchester for beautiful, clean Vancouver, set between mountains and the sea, was a revelation in itself. You could go skiing and play tennis on the same day! I had my own apartment overlooking the beach in Kitsilano and my own car. What could be better? What could go wrong?

So I started work with O'Keefe. I quickly learned that this brewery was part of a string of a dozen brewing plants spread right across Canada and collectively known as Canadian Breweries Limited (CBL). This conglomerate had been assembled by the redoubtable Edward Plunket

(E.P.) Taylor, whose dream was to create "national brands" (Carling Black Label, Red Cap Ale, Old Vienna) and others, which would be uniformly available coast to coast. To do this, he had steadily bought up independent breweries, all of them doing solid business making their own local brands, which he retained as long as they remained profitable. Meanwhile, CBL was introducing its national brands and giving them a strong marketing push. When I joined the company, E.P. had just stepped down as CEO to breed racehorses, among them the famously successful Northern Dancer. There is a film of E.P. in a horse-drawn carriage, driving down the course opening the Queen's Plate race with Queen Elizabeth II as his passenger. As a working-class guy from the industrial north of England, I was unimpressed.

Although the O'Keefe brewery was a streamlined, stainless-steel monument to efficiency, I did wonder about certain things. What, I asked, was this large vessel labelled "cereal cooker" next to the mash mixer? I didn't recognize it from British brewing. "Ah," I was told, "that's where the corn grits are cooked [hydrolyzed] before they're added to the main body of the mash." Corn grits? A light dawned from my Corn Products days. Of course—cornstarch! These were the screenings from a cornstarch production plant in Lincoln, Nebraska, screenings that had been recycled to the breweries. I asked Gerry why we were adding this stuff to "extend the mash" and was told, "It makes the beer lighter in colour, lighter in flavour, and light, light, light, Frank, is the North American style." Really? What he didn't say was that it made the beer cheaper to make, corn grits being about a third the price of barley malt. We were dealing with the bottom line.

To be fair, there was another reason for "diluting" the mash with non-malt cereal: North American barley malt adds about 10 percent more protein to the mash, most of which has to be gotten rid of, otherwise it comes back to haunt you as a cloudy protein haze (chill haze) when the beer is chilled before serving. Beer drinkers drink with their eyes, and when they see haze in the beer when it's opened (after spending perhaps a month on the back porch in a Canadian winter), they conclude that it has "gone off." It hasn't. It's just throwing off a protein haze, the soluble protein having become insoluble at freezing temperatures.

I thought, okay, this is the way they have to do things in frigid Canada, but it still bothered me. Did we have to compromise our recipes to cater to those know-nothing people getting their beer off the porch? Or were we just thinking about the bottom line? Or following the sheep? Were the people of Canada really demanding "light, light, light"? Or was that just what we were pushing—beer that was cheap to produce accompanied by a nationwide barrage of advertising? After all, our competitors—Carling (ostensibly our sister plant in the CBL family but very much a competitor in the marketplace), Labatt and Molson—were cranking out precisely the same kind of beer, practically indistinguishable on the palates of our carefully conducted taste panels. And the amount of corn grits we added to the brew had been growing steadily to above 40 percent of the mash recipe. Where would it end?

There were other compromises too, sacrifices to efficiency of production. When I asked why we didn't make a dark beer, the reply was, "Well, we do make one, but it's a real dog in the marketplace." It was called Gold Label, and it was O'Keefe's standard lager darkened with some caramelized sugar. No kidding it wasn't selling well—you could taste the caramel! It wasn't a brown ale or a porter or a rich *dunkel* lager. It was a fake, a poor attempt that was doomed to failure. But it did save the expense of keeping stores of chocolate malt and roasted barley and having to adjust the malt mill every time you made a batch. In this bright, clean, streamlined plant, everything had been sacrificed to efficiency and cost-effectiveness, including the central thing about beer: how it tastes.

Then there was the pasteurizer, a huge machine that occupied half of the bottling area. It was designed to heat-treat the beer in the bottle by slowly raising the temperature to 140°F (60°C), holding it there for twenty minutes, then slowly cooling it again. This was achieved by spraying warm, then hot, then warm, and finally cool water onto the bottles as they slowly advanced through this monster machine. In this way, you could guarantee that the beer in the bottle was sterile and its shelf life would be infinite. But was it necessary? Most of the beer was consumed within three months of bottling. My plate counts showed that there were rarely any spoilage organisms in the beer delivered to the bottle filler. However, with sixty to a hundred filling heads, bottle fillers were hard to clean, so the pasteurizer had been introduced as the solution to any bugs that might get through. But in a modern plant like this it was overkill: I took swabs regularly from the filling tubes after cleaning, and the results seldom showed any spoilage organisms. And in achieving its infinite shelf life, what was this process doing to the beer? The vitamins in the beer were destroyed by the heating, and we were altering the flavour—for the worse. It was subtle, but with a keen sense of smell and taste, one could pick out the difference between beer before it was pasteurized and after. In brewing texts the post-pasteurized taste is described as "cooked" or "biscuity," and it's amplified by the presence of dissolved oxygen due to air in the beer. This led to dozens of tests for air content being done on our bottled beer every day, while I was thinking, Why are we pasteurizing it at all? If I asked, the usual answer was, "Everybody does it. Molson, Labatt, Carling—everybody."

It's interesting that only a few years later, Coors announced that it had developed a bottling line capable of filling beer bottles with complete sterility and was discontinuing the practice of pasteurizing. Within a decade all the major breweries had followed suit. Today you would be hard-pressed to find a pasteurizer in any brewery.

*

One of the most enervating things about working in a branch plant for a nationwide conglomerate was that all major decisions concerning the product were made at head office—in our case, in Toronto. Our brewmaster had no say in the recipes, brewing methods, labels and package design, or the marketing of the beers. His role was merely to deal with logistics: the procurement of ingredients and supplies, and working out which beers were brewed when and in sufficient quantities to ensure enough finished product some months into the future. What was the point in spending years studying microbiology, biochemistry, brewing-plant design and recipe formulations when none of it was required on the job? It was a sort of Catch-22: you had to have the qualifications to get the job, but once hired you would need only a fraction of this knowledge. Reading the brewing press, I noted that some mega breweries in the States, such as Anheuser-Busch, had already done away with the title of brewmaster for their top production-staff person, substituting "production manager" instead. A less impressive title perhaps, but more honest.

It wasn't long before I discovered that too much knowledge could be a dangerous thing. To add some spice to the boredom of routine testing, I undertook little study projects of my own, wrote them up as technical papers, and some of them were published in the brewing press. Harley, our vice-president, was delighted to see his plant and his quality control supervisor mentioned in print. But through the grapevine I heard that the head of the main lab in Toronto was not pleased that some guy in faraway Vancouver had been published when he and his own staff never had the wit to write anything remotely interesting.

Then one Monday morning the cracks in the edifice of my dream job turned into a yawning chasm. Harley, who had just returned from head office in Toronto, called the staff into his office for a meeting. *The guy was cleaning out his desk!* In response to our astonished looks, he mastered his emotions enough to tell us, "Sorry, folks, but I am no longer with the company." We were dumbstruck. How? Why? For what? To our stumbling questions, our beloved boss could only say that he couldn't comment on it. It was unreal, unbelievable and totally unexpected. The only crumb of an answer came from Ted, our accountant: "Well, I've been with this brewery since it opened five years ago, and it hasn't made a profit yet." I suppose getting rid of the highest-paid guy at the plant made some sense in reducing costs, but it was a gut-wrenching experience for most of us, though only one in a series as it turned out. (I should add that, within a month the highly qualified Harley had been hired by Molson as vice-president of operations in Alberta, a position he occupied until he retired.)

Was it even fair to compare the profitability of our new-kid-on-the-block plant with the money-makers around town? All of them had taken over existing breweries with proven track records. Carling had bought Vancouver Breweries, Molson had bought Sick's Capilano, and Labatt had acquired Lucky Lager in New Westminster and Silver Spring in Victoria. Beers like VB Pilsener, Old Style and Lucky Lager had been established cash cows long before the names of their new corporate masters were added to their labels. What the corporations brought with them were their national brands. Carling Black Label, Molson Canadian and Labatt Blue, even when accompanied by big-time marketing, had been a long time gaining acceptance and nosing out the old favourites. Meanwhile, they had ridden on the coattails of the old, established brands.

Our new plant had no such advantages. It was brand new and its products—O'Keefe's Old Vienna and O'Keefe Ale—were unknown in the West. So it was a bit of an uphill battle from day one. Add to that the burden of amortizing the cost of this showpiece brewery, and you start to see why our plant had been struggling to attain profitability. And Carling, our "big sister plant" across town, which was ostensibly our corporate buddy in CBL, actually started poaching our draft-beer accounts, getting them to switch from O'Keefe to Carling by slipping the barmen twenty-dollar bills, buying rounds and so forth. Sisters indeed!

There must have been more to the axing of Harley than that, I thought. Why would a company fire a guy with so much to offer—handsome, likeable, with a degree in microbiology, a brewing school diploma and an MBA to boot? *Fortune* would have named him "most likely to succeed" as a CEO in the brewing world. Then it hit me: they hadn't fired him in spite of his credentials but because of them. This guy was headed to the top! And there were a number of people among the vice-presidents that E.P. Taylor had surrounded himself with at head office who were uneasy with that because they wanted the top job. Harley's plant still wasn't making a profit after five years? It was a good enough excuse. Dirty corporate politics did Harley in. But he had the satisfaction of seeing many of his old enemies lose their jobs as the entire *Titanic* of CBL started to slip under on the sales charts, a behemoth of a company going nowhere with no new ideas, dead in the water.

3 Uncle Ben Ginter

ABOUT TWO YEARS BEFORE I WAS HIRED BY O'KEEFE, A guy named Benjamin George Ginter bought the old Caribou Brewing Co. and proceeded to give the big boys fits with his antics.

Ginter came from Manitoba. He had been a construction worker, bulldozer driver and heavy-duty mechanic before he started his own construction company with a fleet of trucks and bulldozers and began picking up contracts across Western Canada. In 1950 he chose Prince George as his base, placing him as the go-to guy for building the network of roads throughout the north that were the passion of Social Credit premier W.A.C. Bennett and his highways minister, "Flying Phil" Gaglardi. These three free-enterprise, self-made men became great friends, the government road-building contracts rolled in for Ginter and he made a fortune.

In 1962 the defunct Caribou Brewing Co. plant in Prince George came up for sale. It was owned by CBL, which already had two breweries in the province, Carling and O'Keefe, in Vancouver. It was out of the question to sell the brewing plant to competitors Molson or Labatt, lest they upgrade it and start to take over the beer market in the north. But Ginter was looking for warehouse space and made an offer of $150,000. CBL decided to accept his offer: "A truck driver? What the hell would he know about beer?"

But Ginter hired himself an Austrian brewmaster and, with support from the hotels of Prince George, launched his beer on the market. He had no hesitation about giving his brands names that were very similar to those of the big favourites in the US, such as "Budd," "High Life" and "Paap's," but when threats of lawsuits started to come from the big boys in the States, he decided to call his beer Tartan. His labels featured a picture of him—a big, brawny, smiling, bearded guy wearing a plaid shirt with logger suspenders. The working man's brewery owner! The beer quickly became known as Uncle Ben's. And it was just different enough from the major brands to pique the people's interest—a little darker, with more malt, less corn adjunct and a little more positive hop.

When Carling had sold its old Creston brewery to Kai Jakobsen, a former CBL old boy, it had made a deal with him that the big boys would not market their beers in the Kootenays and Kai would sell his beer there and nowhere else in BC. So began a curious time when, once you crossed the mountain passes from the Okanagan into the Kootenays, you couldn't find a bottle of Carling, Molson or Labatt, and the only beer available was Kokanee or Kootenay Ale. But when CBL tried to make a similar deal with Ginter, he would have nothing to do with it, so in no time his beer was for sale in the Lower Mainland to curious customers and increasing sales. The big guys shook their heads.

One day in the late 1960s, Gerry, the brewmaster at O'Keefe, came into the lab and said, "Hey Frank, Uncle Ben is giving a talk at BCIT. You want to go?" I was intrigued. BCIT was only minutes from O'Keefe, and off we went in Gerry's car. Nobody there knew either of us and we had never met Ginter, so we could be safely incognito. As we stood in the lineup to get into the hall, I noticed the queue was mostly male students. Some were carrying bags of Uncle Ben's bottle caps. I got talking to the guy ahead of us in line, and what he said left us speechless: "That's what's required for admission: a dozen Uncle Ben's beer caps." *A dozen Uncle Ben's beer caps!* Carling O'Keefe poured tens of thousands of dollars into promotion, but nobody had ever come up with anything like this, and it hadn't cost Ginter a cent—in fact, it had made him some extra cents. Gerry and I stumbled out of the line and had a quick confab in the parking lot. "Well," he said, "now I really want to hear this SOB." There was a liquor store nearby, so we zoomed over to it, bought two cases of Uncle Ben's, hid behind a building, where we removed the caps and left the beer behind, no doubt providing a nice surprise for someone. A little breathless, we went back to the hall, gave our caps to the curious guy at the door and went in to hear Uncle Ben.

His talk was not memorable. It was a freewheeling tribute to free enterprise and the self-made man—him. He styled himself as the little guy battling the biggies while his sole motivation was to bring good, honest beer to working men, people like himself. He made much of his roustabout truck-driving days and told us he wasn't afraid of going toe-to-toe with the Big Three. In fact, he said that since his market share kept growing, he was planning to build a large brewery in the Lower Mainland, plus a string of others across Canada. Gerry and I looked at each other, eyebrows raised.

*

Throughout the 1960s, the Carling O'Keefe, Molson and Labatt plants in the Lower Mainland were besieged by troops of salesmen selling cans and canning lines. It was the upcoming thing, they insisted, and all the rage in the US. They said that cans were cheaper than bottles, and cans meant no more dealing with those smelly returnable bottles and giant bottle washers. Sterility was guaranteed because the new cans were made right on the spot. Customers loved them because they're light, they don't break and you can throw 'em in the back of the truck.

It seems strange now, but the Big Three had perfectly logical reasons for not going into cans. First, a canning line was going to cost half a million dollars and their entire brewery packaging areas would have to be redesigned. Second, what would they gain? Between them they controlled over 90 percent of the beer market, split more or less evenly, and the overall beer market was not going to increase just because the beer came in cans. Of course, if one of the three went for cans, the other two would have to follow suit because of the market advantage cans would give, but after they had all switched to cans, paid for the equipment and the dust had settled, they would likely still have the same three-way split and no increase in profit. Therefore, the Big Three—in all their plants right across Canada—had an unwritten agreement that they were not going into cans. Of course, their game didn't allow for the joker in the pack.

When word spread through the O'Keefe plant that Ginter was putting in a canning line, we didn't know whether to laugh in disbelief or ask ourselves how he could do it. We knew he couldn't possibly have afforded it, and where would he get the technical help? The answer was the canning companies, of course. They had given him an open-ended lease-to-own agreement that cost him next to nothing, and they provided the tech backup free "to see if he liked it." Ginter loved it. In no time at all, he had the first and only canned beer available in the Lower Mainland market, and by the summer of 1966 Tartan beer in cans had 7 percent of the beer market. The Big Three reluctantly ordered their canning lines.

What sank Ginter's ride on the beer wave was not so much the big boys but massively overextending himself by buying up suitable brewery sites in BC, Alberta and Manitoba and wheeling and dealing with the Ontario government over a site in Cornwall that came to nothing. He even approached Joey Smallwood with a plan to establish the first brewery in Newfoundland, but this fell through when Smallwood demanded ten cents for each case sold. Debts and lawsuits started to pile up. There were also problems with the unions, which he wouldn't allow in his workforce. This had worked in Prince George, but in the Lower Mainland he was up against the Brewery Workers' Union, the Teamsters and the construction unions. Ginter's brewery site in Richmond was picketed from day one, and the construction slowdown stretched into months and years. In 1976 the bank presented him with a demand note for $3.9 million, and when he was unable to pay, they foreclosed. His business was paralyzed, and he was forced to sell the Prince George brewery and his heavy equipment fleet, the unfinished brewery in Richmond, another in Red Deer, and the warehouse that was supposed to become his Winnipeg plant.

In 1982 Ginter announced that he had repaid all his debts. That same year he suffered two heart attacks, the second putting him in the hospital, where he died. He was fifty-nine.

4 | Decline and Fall

AFTER HARLEY DEEKS WAS INVITED TO LEAVE O'KEEFE, his large ground-floor office remained empty, a reminder of the hole where our operation had been kicked in the gut. No replacement was sent, and we were given to understand that we were now to answer to the general manager of the Carling plant at 12th and Vine in Kitsilano. With the rumours of Carling sales reps poaching O'Keefe draft accounts having turned out to be true, relations between the two plants were at their lowest. Now you may as well have told us we had to answer to Labatt or Molson.

Management at the Carling plant didn't inspire any confidence either. The general manager's aim seemed to be keeping the status quo as static as possible, quite the opposite of the dynamic Harley. But to the top execs in Toronto, a manager with no larger ambition than to see his time out until he could retire on a fat pension was ideal. The fellow had no background in brewing and how he got the job was beyond me, but I suspected that he had been a buddy of our founder, E.P. Taylor. I was destined to become something of a thorn in the side of this harmless old gent.

To add insult to injury, O'Keefe had finally come up with a winner. Someone back east had heard our cries of "Why are we always going light, lighter, lightest? How about going back to an all-malt beer? Maybe something stronger, something with robust flavour?" The result was O'Keefe's Extra Old Stock, all-malt with 5.6 percent alcohol (wow!). This break with the slide to imitate Budweiser, Coors and Miller Lite was a surprise success. Real beer drinkers rallied around it, and it became known as "High Test." Note to beer marketers: if you can come up with a brand that's unique, that grabs the attention of consumers so that a slogan for it arises not from the sales department but from the public itself, you're on to something. Such was the case with "High Test." It took off, carving out a chunk of the beer market as no new product had done in years.

Extra Old Stock could have been the product that turned things around for our plant, but instead just as we were about to launch it, the invisible powers that be back east decided to move our entire bottling operation to the Carling plant, so Carling got the benefit of this windfall. I can recall our bottle shop supervisor, Mike, a huge mountain of a man, with tears in his eyes after he was told that he would be transferred back east. He had seen our state-of-the-art plant built and been with the operation from day one. He loved the brewery and Vancouver.

It was hard not to dwell on what was happening to our wonderful showpiece brewery and to my job. The beautiful gardens were no longer maintained, and slowly the front-office staff and salesmen were let go or sifted off to the Carling plant. Our chief engineer went there too, to be followed in due course by Gerry, our brewmaster. In time

I was the only white-collar worker in the place, with an entire office block to myself.

Once again I turned to writing to divert my gloomy thoughts. I had lost all interest in writing technical brewing papers, which might have given me more problems with the main lab, and I decided to try more widespread subjects, including the social phenomenon of the large number of American draft dodgers then flooding into Vancouver to avoid having to fight in the Vietnam War. In 1968 protests against the war were frequent, and many of the rallies took place around the newly opened fountain plaza of the Vancouver courthouse. The mayor of Vancouver, Tom "Terrific" Campbell, was very proud of his new plaza, so when he saw it being claimed as a hangout for these "undesirables" with their long hair, dubious lifestyle and political motives, he was not happy. Who he wanted was nice, middle-class workers enjoying themselves on their lunch hour. A former lawyer, he came up with an answer by digging out an obscure section of the Public Works Act added during World War II and designed to prevent subversive-looking types from hanging around public buildings. It gave police the authority to ask "undesirables" who frequented the plaza to move on and, if they failed to comply, to arrest and jail them.

This offended many Vancouverites' sense of social justice. How exactly were the police supposed to select those to whom they might give "the bum's rush"? On the basis of their long hair? Or perhaps because they were protesting an unjust and insupportable war? The BC Civil Liberties Association was vocal in pointing out that that section of the act had never been designed for such use and should have been struck off the books long ago. I decided to write a piece about this situation, and it was published in *Saturday Night* magazine. It was not kind to Tom Terrific. I was pleased that a respected nationwide magazine had thought it important enough to report on what was obviously a misuse of a bylaw, but one day when I returned to work from lunch, our one remaining front-office person gave me a curious look.

"Is it you?" she asked.

"Of course it's me," I said. "Who did you think it was?"

"No," she said, "are you the Frank Appleton that they're talking about on the radio, the one who wrote this article that the mayor is going to sue over?"

Ho, ho, I thought. It's me.

After finding out that the mayor's reaction to my article had indeed been to say he was going to sue me and the magazine, I put in a call to *Saturday Night* and asked to speak to Arnold Edinborough, the editor. To my surprise, there he was. It was the first time we had spoken. After I gave my briefing on the doings in Vancouver, he was more than supportive. He was jovial.

"This man is a lawyer?" he said. "No wonder he became mayor! Listen, my boy, everything that appears in this magazine is read by our lawyers, who alert me to possible lawsuits. I see one has written on your piece 'demonstrable performance.' You know what that means?" I told him I didn't.

"Demonstrable performance means that you are able to demonstrate that what you wrote is demonstrably true, that it can be backed up by the facts. Now, Frank, can you vouch to me that everything you wrote in that piece is true?"

"Of course," I said. "Pretty well everything is in the public record."

"That's what I thought," Edinborough replied. "It's just bluster from a rooster whose feathers have been ruffled. If he is unwise enough to go to court, our Vancouver lawyers will be only too happy to oblige. He will lose, lose face, and have to pay all the costs."

I hated to cut into Edinborough's good mood, but I had another problem. "Yes," I said, "but I also have this job with a brewery..."

"You have? Hmmm...and they might give you grief?" There was silence while Edinborough pondered. Then he said, "Well, my friend, you might be out of a job with the brewery, but you've got a great start in journalism!"

And that was that. After days of trepidation, no more threats came from Tom Terrific, and everything started to die down. Except with Mr. Round. He was simmering with anger that this minor lab guy had the impertinence to attract the ire of no less than the mayor of Vancouver. And to do it in a magazine highly regarded back east, a magazine published in Toronto, no less! So I was called to a meeting in his office across town. I think he was more nervous than I was. The scene went something like this:

> ROUND: (*stabbing a copy of the magazine with his finger*) This has got to stop! *This has got to stop!* I can't have an employee embarrassing the company like this!
>
> APPLETON: Embarrassing? How? There can't be more than a handful of people who would connect the Appleton who wrote that piece with the O'Keefe quality-control guy.
>
> ROUND: There will be a lot more! The mayor is going to *sue you!*

APPLETON: It's all bluster! I've talked to the editor, and he has consulted his lawyers and they say Campbell doesn't have a leg to stand on. Like I say in the article, he's misusing not a law but an ancient *bylaw* to clear perfectly law-abiding folk from a public place. It's an unconscionable misuse of his office, and the magazine and its lawyers are standing behind me.

ROUND: They are? Oh my God! A *court case*! It'll be in all the papers...

APPLETON: It will never happen! Haven't you been reading the local papers? They're all after him for expropriating the law for his own ends. He'll have to cave in.

ROUND: So you say. We'll wait and see. Listen, Frank (*giving me a warning look*). I think you need to give some thought to whether you want to keep your position with us or take up your journalism. If you want to stay with us, I want you to sign a document saying that *any* writing you do for publication must be approved by me first. (*Reaching for the intercom*) I'll get my secretary to draw it up right now, and she can witness it.

APPLETON: I won't sign it.

ROUND: (*incredulous*) What?

APPLETON: I already signed a confidentiality agreement when I started with this company. I have a copy of it here. It states that if I write anything concerning the company, its products, methods, or processes, anything that might be considered confidential company information, such writing has to be approved by my superiors before submission. It says nothing about any writing not concerning the company. I intend to keep to that agreement. Anything concerning beer, processes, the company, et cetera will be submitted for your approval. Anything else will not. Here's a copy of that document. It is countersigned by Harley Deeks.

ROUND: Harley Deeks is no longer with the company!

APPLETON: Unfortunately that is so. Harley was quite pleased with my efforts at getting published in the brewing press. I wonder what he would have thought about me sticking up for the little guy in a battle with the slick lawyer that is our mayor? Anyway, I am not about to let you censor my work when it has nothing to do with the company.

ROUND: I think you are walking on thin ice, Frank.

APPLETON: Well, you could always fire me. But I wonder what reasons you would give. Insubordination? Saying things about our sharp mayor that are demonstrably true?

ROUND: (*miserably, looking at me with a sad, perplexed expression*) I could fire you. Bear that in mind. That is all.

I waited to see what would follow. As predicted, the answer was…nothing. There were no more outbursts from Tom Campbell, that section of the Public Works Act was quietly dropped, and life returned to normal on the plaza. At O'Keefe, "returned to normal" for me meant that I wasn't fired, but I was left in a sort of lonely limbo, "frozen out" as they say. No internal company communications came to me, and since phone calls went through the Carling switchboard, calls for me became almost non-existent. And now that we were just "the kegging plant," with no bottling operation to keep tabs on, my job was easier if anything, but it was a sad way for it all to end.

Sometimes being the lone worker in the whole office block had its comic aspects, as on the day I heard the front doorbell ringing, followed by a lusty banging on the door. With the removal of the last receptionist in the office, there was nobody to check visitors, and as we didn't do tours anymore, the door was kept locked at all times, with a notice for tradesmen to use the brewery side entrance. Still, the banging and ringing kept up until I had to descend from the second-floor laboratory to see what it was all about. There was a middle-aged man in a suit whose face looked annoyed though slightly familiar. Had I seen it in a brewing monthly? Of course! It was the CEO of Canadian Breweries Ltd. on a swing out west to check on his far-flung operations.

"Ah, you must be Frank," he said, shaking my hand. He looked a little flustered. "What the hell is going on here?" he demanded. "Why is the door locked? Why is there no staff here?"

I explained that all the secretarial staff had either been let go or sent to the Carling plant.

"The cheap bastards!" he exclaimed. "Nobody left to answer the front door! Unbelievable!"

But I'm thinking, *Just a minute, who are these "cheap bastards" he's talking about? This guy is the CEO, and he doesn't know what's been going on here for the past year or more?* Mr. Round, who was standing behind him, could have informed him but had said nothing. Instead he was watching me closely in case I came out with anything embarrassing. At that point I decided that this was just the CEO's way of fumbling through an awkward situation. I brought him through the empty office block and the brewery with him shaking his head and muttering, "This will never do. This is no good." He even spent a few minutes listening to my take on the forced decline of our plant compared to that of the Carling plant and promised that things would improve. But they didn't. It was all fakery.

After he left, things went on just as before—with the front door locked. I never saw him again. And he was gone from the top job pretty soon. The reason was yet another revelation: in 1969, Canadian Breweries Ltd. was sold to Rothmans, the tobacco giant. I hadn't realized it, but not only our plant but pretty much the entire CBL operation was in trouble, flatlining on the sales graphs. The Canadian population was expanding at a rate of 5 percent per year, but the great ship CBL was just afloat at zero percent growth. Unless we expanded sales 5 percent every year, we were going to sink.

With the sale to Rothmans, we had executives with curious English/South African accents checking out the breweries and looking for answers while offering us packs of cigarettes! I've never had a taste for tobacco and did my best to refuse politely while I was showing them around. One of them was quite young, in his thirties like me, and was very interested in my ideas for new products. As a bit of a joke, I said, "What about kaffir beer?"

"Kaffir beer?" he said. "Over here?"

Kaffir beer, which is well known in South Africa, is a traditional beer made by grinding kaffir corn and malt and fermenting the mash. It had been adopted by some sizable breweries in South Africa but was mainly consumed by the black populations in the Bantu and Zulu homelands.

"Do you really think it would go over here?" he asked.

"Well," I said, "the beers we're making now are 40 percent cornstarch."

He was intrigued by that and said that, if I would write my suggestions down, he would bring them to the attention of the board of directors back east. I smiled inwardly, wondering what the reaction would be, but I never heard any more about *that* either. However, not long after that, when CBL was sold yet again, this time to Elders, the Aussie brewing giant, someone found my letters proposing the making of alternative products when they were cleaning out the desk of the Rothmans executive. That's when I was told by Mr. Round to cease and desist writing directly to top executives and to submit any further ideas "through the proper channels." Good luck with that, I told myself. My ideas were now effectively muzzled.

The final piece of the O'Keefe puzzle fell into place in 1972, when it was announced that our plant would be closing for good within a year. Despite the fact that the gathering clouds had been looming for some time, I was still angry. I was told that a position was available for me at the Carling plant—as the number two guy in the lab. It was, in fact, a demotion, since my qualifications and background, not to mention the past year of single-handedly overseeing brewing and production at O'Keefe, demanded better. It was the final squeeze play of the game. If they fired me with no real grounds—for example, incompetence or damage to the company—I would be eligible for severance pay, which after eight years of service would be quite a sum. But if I didn't eat crow and refused to take the job offered, quitting instead, they wouldn't have to shell out a cent.

I wrote a scathing letter to the president and posted copies on the notice boards in both plants. They were taken down and shredded by management, but not soon enough: a number of copies were circulated "underground" by junior staff and workers. And I walked out, thinking I would never return to the brewing business again.

One really nice thing happened to lighten my gloom. A couple of weeks after I quit, my friend Stan, a maintenance man at O'Keefe who had shared rides to work with me, called to say there was to be a dinner and some sort of social at the Walnut Grove Community Centre in Langley, near where we both lived, and that I really must attend. It would brighten my dark mood, said Stan. So off we went. When I walked into the room, I saw many familiar faces beaming at me: the blue-collar workers from the O'Keefe plant! They had organized a surprise send-off party for me. I had come to know them well in recent years. During my trips down the freeway into Burnaby with Stan, I had mentioned that I'd bought 20 acres of treed hillside in a remote valley in the Kootenays, and if the bottom fell out of my job, I was going to "drop out" and homestead there. Stan was fascinated by the idea, since he had grown up near Riske Creek in the Cariboo. He had fond memories of the freedom of life in rural BC, wistfully contrasting it with the hustling, money-driven Lower Mainland. So he had asked for contributions from his workmates to give me a start in my new life, not of money but of *tools*. There, up on the stage at the end of the hall, was a wonderful collection of axes, hammers, ropes and pulley blocks, a peavey, saws, logging chains, a froe for splitting shakes, an adze, wedges, oil lamps, a coffee pot, pots and pans—a great collection of useful stuff. I was overwhelmed.

One by one, the guys came up, shook my hand and thanked me for my stand against the Carling management in trying to keep our plant open. It was an emotional evening I will never forget.

5 The Sinking of the Great Ship CBL

AT THE BEGINNING OF THE 1960S, CANADIAN BREWERIES Ltd. had twelve breweries across Canada, acquired through buyouts by that master of the brewery monopoly game, E.P. Taylor. His company had become the dominant player in the Big Three—CBL, Labatt and Molson. But in a secret deal in 1968 Taylor had sold his controlling interest in CBL to Rothmans, and his grand design of creating a national brewing empire from coast to coast came to an end. In fact, the giant company he sold was ailing, and today his much-vaunted national brands—Carling Black Label, O'Keefe's Old Vienna, Dow, Red Cap Ale—have mostly disappeared from store shelves, and those left are now brewed by Molson Coors.

When a huge company finds its sales languishing, there is no shortage of senior management people pushing ideas on what to do next. In the case of CBL most of their ideas were financially disastrous, and the company suffered through them all.

Taylor's vanity brewery in the Bahamas

E.P. himself was responsible for the first of these disasters. He had a tax-haven home in the Bahamas, and though plenty of good international brands—Heineken, Guinness, Carlsberg, Bass—were available there, few American labels and no Canadian ones were on the shelves. He decided what Nassau needed was a brewery to brew *his* beer: Carling Black Label. It would be his own pet brewery. There were a couple of problems with this plan, however, the first being the cost of constructing an entire brewing plant way off in the Caribbean, and the second being the ongoing costs of providing it with malted barley and other ingredients. But E.P.'s engineers and brewmasters came up with an ingenious plan to use an underutilized brewery in Montreal to brew the wort for the beer, concentrate it into a thick malt syrup, pack it into giant rubber bags and ship them to Nassau. Once there, all the local labour had to do was dilute the concentrated malt extract, add yeast, wait for it to ferment, store it for a while, filter and bottle it. As every brewmaster knows, there is a bit more to good beer than that. No extract beer I've ever met tasted exactly like the ground-malt mash original. This is because of the excessive heat treatment the wort endures in evaporating it to a syrup. It changes the biochemical makeup of the wort, the flavour dynamic.

The brewery was also hit with quality control problems because the whale-sized rubber bags that held the malt syrup turned out to be a nightmare to clean, leaving behind some attractive soup in which vile organisms could prosper in the Caribbean sun. When the bags were returned to Montreal, they stank. How do you clean and sterilize the inside of a collapsed balloon? The beer produced was nowhere near the quality of the well-known European imports, and the brewery closed down—with significant losses—after about a year.

Carling invades the us: How the American Southwest was *not* won

By the early 1960s Molson, Labatt and New Brunswick's Moosehead had been making modest gains in the eastern us market, but all of their beer was made in Canada and distributed through a variety of agents on the other side of the line. CBL decided to do them one—or two—better. The company would build two brand-new plants, one in Fort Worth, Texas, the other in Phoenix, Arizona—which is not noted for its water quality—to produce Carling beers and take the American beer scene by storm. The southwest was chosen because it was an untapped market—or so the CBL executive thought—but it was also an untried market that was completely unfamiliar with Carling beer. The brands that dominated the area were Coors, Budweiser and Miller, all well-established, powerful competition. Unfazed by these realities, crews of engineers, brewmasters and technicians were dispatched from Ontario to create showpiece breweries. The one in Texas was interesting from a brewing technology standpoint because it was the first in North America to use a continuous brewing system in which the beer was produced by moving it steadily through a series of tower-like vessels instead of using the usual batch-wise process. This had been tried successfully in New Zealand but never in North America. By the time it opened in 1964 the Fort Worth plant had cost $8 million US and had been voted one of the best-designed plants in America. Within a year it was closed due to dismal sales; it was sold off for $5.5 million. The new 300,000-barrel-capacity Phoenix plant was offloaded the same year for $4.5 million.

What kind of thinking was going on here? Test-marketing of your products is an essential when you are thinking of moving into unknown territory, but so sure of success were the CBL executives that they seem to have ignored test-marketing entirely. The unknown Carling brands were met with indifference by Americans, and sales were pitiful. To add to the problem, successful results from a continuous brewing system depend on keeping the beer moving. Stops and starts produce variable results in the quality of the beer. The joke in the industry was that Carling had perfected a continuous brewing system but was unable to find any continuous drinkers. And so ended the disastrous attempt by Carling to win the southwest.

Dow's cobalt scandal

One morning in 1966 I was listening to the radio while getting ready for work at O'Keefe when an item on the news stopped me in my tracks. The announcer said that the Dow Brewery in Quebec City had been implicated in the premature deaths of sixteen men who had died from degenerative heart disease. A doctor studying the deaths had found that all of the men had been heavy drinkers of Dow beer, drinking sixteen pints or more a day. Apparently the brewery had been adding a cobalt compound to improve the head on the beer. Cobalt! A heavy metal! What were these people thinking? I couldn't believe it.

Dow, which had breweries in Ontario and Quebec, was owned by CBL, so I hurried to my job at O'Keefe, hoping there had been some mistake. There hadn't. I had never heard of adding cobalt to beer and would have walked straight out the door if anyone had suggested doing it. As it was, I wasn't happy that we were adding small amounts of sodium alginate (a seaweed derivative widely used in the food industry) to our beer for that same reason—to improve the head. It's a dishonest practice, an admission that you have gone too far in the replacement of malt with adjunct (added junk?) like cornstarch, corn syrup and rice. It also means that you are over-filtering your beer, and you've removed the non-fermentable carbohydrates and soluble proteins that increase the surface tension and produce the nice, tight head in naturally brewed beers made from malted barley. With beers made only from malt, hops, water and yeast and brewed naturally, you don't need to add anything to improve the head. So the use of heading compounds is an indication of brewing chemistry gone off the rails: you are replacing something that never should have been removed in the first place. As for adding something containing *cobalt*? Had anyone thought of the reaction if this came out? And now it had.

People stopped drinking Dow beer, and in an effort to slow the disastrous slide, Dow's marketing team took out full-page ads in Quebec newspapers to announce that despite tests showing nothing was wrong with the company's beer, all stocks of Dow Ale were to be dumped into the St. Lawrence River and all tanks thoroughly cleaned. Something like a million gallons of beer worth $625,000 was dumped, but dumping it only convinced consumers that there really must have been something wrong with it.

Dow was ordered to stop adding cobalt to the beer, and no new cases of degenerative heart disease were reported. Later a government inquiry revealed that there was no direct link between Dow beer and the deaths after all, but the damage had been done. Dow was permanently branded as "chemical beer" and the company never recovered. Dow plants languished due to pathetic sales and eventually closed. In 1973 the breweries were bought at fire-sale prices by Molson.

The keg bottle fiasco

In 1962 the Big Three agreed to standardize their variously shaped bottles to a single type: the stubby. It wasn't that attractive but it was hard to knock over, and having a standard bottle meant the breweries saved money by not having to sort and store a variety of sizes and shapes. Then suddenly in May 1970 CBL announced the launching of a new brand, Heidelberg (a name conjured from Heineken and Carlsberg, perhaps?) in an entirely new package: a keg-shaped bottle with a twist-off cap. Molson and Labatt were quick to pounce on this move as breaking the eight-year agreement. There was quite rightly a feeling that a fresh proliferation of bottle shapes would increase the brewers' costs, not to mention complicating the bottle return program. CBL responded that there had never been an agreement on bottle shapes, and the company carried on with its launch of Heidelberg in Ontario. Sales figures for the new beer—read "new bottle"—were so good that soon the brand was made available in Quebec, Alberta and BC as well, and within a year Heidelberg was selling at close to 10 percent of the market in those areas.

But by that time provincial liquor boards were adding to the pressure from Molson and Labatt for the removal of the keg bottles because of the fear that the increase of bottle shapes would hinder recycling and lead to more litter. When provincial governments ordered the keg bottle to be discontinued, CBL had to comply. Heidelberg was now filled into the same old stubby bottle as all the other beers, and its market share immediately fell below 4 percent— proof once more that consumers "drink with their eyes." Not long after that, the brand was dropped for good. The destruction of the Heidelberg bottles, labels and cartons, not to mention the giant marketing campaign to launch the brand and the retooling of bottling equipment, cost CBL an estimated $1.4 million.

The (failed) invasion of Britain

With breweries now coast to coast, the obvious place for E.P. to expand his empire was across the Atlantic to that great beer-loving land, the UK. It must have been a source of great interest to him that a few of the honourable members of the House of Lords—the Peerage—had been dubbed "the Beerage" by the press, since that was how they had made the fortunes that had funded the political party in power, which had obligingly given them titles.

E.P. decided that what this land of arcane pubs serving variable ales needed was—you guessed it—Carling Black Label! Clear, cold, fizzy and exactly the same in every pub.

("Hey Mabel! Black Label!" got my vote as the most irritating jingle of 1967.) But this fizzy, clear, cold lager did gain a certain acceptance among the young, who were busy rebelling against the old, established order, with its tepid, flat beer. Witness Ringo Starr ordering a round for the guys in *A Hard Day's Night*: "Two pints of lager, please... And... two more pints of lager." Keg beer (as opposed to the old "barrel beer") was a hit—and it still is. Most beers, including craft beers, are still sold that way—from stainless-steel kegs under pressure by carbon dioxide. The problem is not really the method of packaging, but the quality and integrity of the beer in the keg.

E.P. arranged a partnership with one of Britain's largest brewing conglomerates, Bass Charrington Limited, to produce and market Black Label in the UK. Bass Charrington owned 11,000 pubs in the UK and Ireland, the so-called "tied houses" that only served the brands of their owners, so a market for Black Label and other bland lagers was guaranteed. But as these bland brands proliferated throughout the pubs, a backlash began. Older beer drinkers didn't like their favourite ales being pushed out of the pubs by this frigid, fizzy, insipid lager. This "Canadianizing" of the beer scene was viewed as an insult to their favourite tipple, and Black Label was in the centre of their sights.

Something had to be done, and one day four journalists sat down in a pub in Kerry, Ireland, and came up with a plan. It was called the Campaign for Real Ale (CAMRA), and within a year it had spread across the UK, stirring up one of the largest consumer-driven protest movements ever seen there. "We want real ale" was their cry, and a rash of new small breweries and brewpubs answered with the real stuff. Instead of taking over the pub scene in Britain, Black Label was given a black eye, and ironically the Carling brand and its ilk were responsible for the backlash that produced the Real Ale movement, which eventually spread to Canada and provided the impetus for the foundation of the first brewpubs and microbreweries here. It's funny to think that E.P. Taylor's plan for the invasion of Britain by Canadian adjunct lager actually resulted in Canada being invaded by real ale.

When E.P. had sold his controlling interest in CBL to Rothmans in 1968, the wily old "wizard of Bay Street" got $12 for each of his shares, when the market value had already slumped to $9.50. The new parent company then sold off CBL's Bass Charrington holdings, and the Carling brand all but disappeared in the UK.

The (failed) invasion of Asia

As a final note on the reasons for CBL's demise, I'll mention the company's very brief attempt in the mid-1960s to tap into the Asian market by establishing a Carling brewery in Hong Kong. It was one of those CBL specialties of the time: opening a new plant and closing it in little more than a year.

The last post

Even as late as 1977 CBL (rechristened Carling O'Keefe after the loss of Dow) was listed in Michael Jackson's *World Guide to Beer* as the tenth largest brewing company in the world. But in the late 1980s the company became a pawn in the game of corporate brewing mega mergers. In 1987 the Australian conglomerate Elders announced it had acquired 95 percent of Carling O'Keefe's stock through the purchase of Rothmans' 50.1 percent share plus a massive buyout of common stock for a total of $392 million. In the early E.P. Taylor days, the company had been over 90 percent Canadian-owned; the new CEO, Edward Kunkel, said, "This move identifies Carling as a subsidiary of Elders." Oh, how the mighty had fallen—to be reduced to ownership by the Aussies.

However, this new ownership did not last long. Elders thought it would take the Canadian market by storm with its own big brand, Foster's Lager, now brewed by Carling O'Keefe. The advertising starred Paul Hogan of *Crocodile Dundee* fame as the pitchman. But after an initial flurry of sales, the brand languished. It was, after all, just another fizzy, cold, flavourless lager. Discouraged by this, Elders decided to sell or trade all its Canadian holdings, and in July 1989 it was announced that Molson was the new owner, making the Molson conglomerate the number one brewing concern in Canada, with 53 percent of the market. The Big Three had become the Big Two, a move that meant duplication of the Molson and Carling O'Keefe plants in many Canadian cities. To rationalize its operation, Molson closed seven plants, putting some two thousand workers on the streets. The iconic O'Keefe plant in Montreal was closed, as were all the old CBL plants across the West, including Carling in Vancouver, our old nemesis, which had pillaged the O'Keefe brands when I worked there.

Sic transit gloria mundi—Thus passes the glory of the world.

6

Homesteading, Writing and... John Mitchell

LEAVING VANCOUVER FOR THE WILDS OF THE KOOTENAYS was both scary and exhilarating. Scary because I had no job or income, exhilarating because a great weight had been lifted from my shoulders after my trials with the CBL hierarchy. I was free of it. And I was starting on a great adventure to explore life in this great land, Canada, and carve out my little niche in it. It was a dream that dated back to reading about this immense country when I was still a boy in England, but I had been living here for nine years and had seen only glimpses of it, since most of my time had been spent inside a brewery. Now I would realize my dream! My parents had paid rent on a humble brick row house in Manchester for over twenty years and never succeeded in owning it. That was not going to happen to me. I would build my own house with local materials in the beautiful Inonoaklin Valley. No bosses, no rent, no mortgage. Free!

There were no buildings on my rocky, treed hillside. Nothing at all. It was classed as "wild land" and the taxes were all of $7.50 a year at that time. There was no overhead, but no services either. However, the BC Hydro line followed the road next to my property, and pure mountain streams ran down the hillside behind me.

So I set about falling trees and building a house. The work was hard but enjoyable. I had never before run a chainsaw, dug a trench or manhandled rocks, but these jobs were all necessary to create an open space for my first tiny cabin and garden. All that work gave me a wonderful appetite, and at night I slept like a contented baby. If I wondered why I was doing all this, all I had to do was lift my head and enjoy the snow-capped mountains of the Valhalla Range and breathe in the country air scented with wildflowers. No doubt about it, I had found my home. This would be where I made my stand. And I am still here and will be until the spark of life gives out.

Making a living was another issue. The jobs available in the valley were pretty basic: working in the bush for one of the logging outfits or on the one large local dairy farm; the best jobs were on the Highways Department crew or on the ferry that shuttled back and forth across Lower Arrow Lake. None of these appealed to me. Meanwhile, my appearance in the valley, determinedly putting down roots in a place where everyone seemed to be related, attracted some attention.

"What you goin' to do with that piece of land?" asked an old widowed farmer who had taken a shine to this curiosity with the educated vocabulary. "You can't farm it. It's all stood up on end!"

I couldn't argue with this pronouncement.

"You goin' to work out in the bush?"

I shook my head and explained that I'd had some success in writing and getting published in magazines, and my plan was to expand my writing talents into a freelance career.

"You can make money at that?" he asked, incredulous.

Despite this, he very kindly invited me over for a meal and the opportunity to have a shower, a nice gesture since I had no bathing facilities. I soon learned that he didn't play chess, but he could whip me at checkers.

Still, even with very little overhead, I did need some cash for basics: groceries, hardware for the building project, gas and oil for my little truck, chainsaws and oil lamps and so forth. I wrote about anything and everything I could think of and supplemented the end products with photographs I took myself. While the subject matter in this remote valley was pretty limited, I used my biology background to write on birds, bugs, beekeeping and butterflies, as well as skiing, mountaineering, canoe trips and the history of the area, which had been opened up by gold and silver miners only a century earlier. In those days the highways into the area had been the network of lakes, hundreds of miles long, which had been traversed by a fleet of paddlewheelers: more grist for my mill.

My first breakthrough came when I had an idea for writing a piece on a local tree-planting crew. If this had been your usual tree-planting crew, mostly male, it might not have stirred much interest, but this was an all-female crew, supervised by a local male forester. My publishing goal was *Weekend Magazine,* a full-colour Saturday supplement that appeared in most of the major daily papers across Canada. It was a general-interest magazine that was read mainly by women. I went out on a day's planting expedition with the crew and wrote the story from their point of view. In this case my story hook was what this all-female crew had to say about the job and why they were out there. "Raising a Forest From the Dead" started like this: "After their husbands, the loggers, have cut down the trees and left, the next year their wives gather on the mountainside to plant the tiny seedlings which will give birth to a new forest." How could any woman resist the analogy? The final touch was added by the German/Canadian overseer of the crew. When I asked him why he liked working with the crew, he replied, "Because women don't bitch!" It was the perfect quote; the editor at *Weekend Magazine* loved it! When it appeared, the reaction in our valley was astonishment and disbelief, though there were a few sour comments from the loggers. This unusual stranger, Appleton, had put them on the map in a Canada-wide magazine! My own reaction when I got a cheque for $750—this was 1975!—and a note from the editor that he wanted to see more of my work was about equally disbelieving. It was twice what I had been getting from magazines in BC.

This initial effort led to several years of contributions to *Weekend Magazine*. The subjects ranged from the pros and cons of building a geodesic dome to falcons and falconry, a story that centred on Frank Beebe, the illustrator for the Royal BC Museum's iconic natural history handbooks. The peppery Beebe kept peregrine falcons and was quite acerbic about no-nothing naturalists who wanted the sport banned. While falconry wasn't the kind of subject matter that *Weekend* usually accepted, the outspoken Beebe gave the story all the human interest I needed. Other times, my science background helped me write about detecting fetal birth defects, the implications of the baby boom as it rolled on through the years, beekeeping, dragonflies, stinging insects, and wild edible mushrooms. As I got to be a regular with *Weekend*, the editors began to suggest story ideas to me. One of these—a bit of a caper, really—was probably inspired by the popularity of Euell Gibbons's book *Stalking the Wild Asparagus*, which was about the joys of finding wild edible food while rambling about in nature. The editors set me a challenge: Could I come up with a meal of free, natural ingredients within Greater Vancouver? I couldn't turn down the challenge. I based myself at my sister Charlie's place in the city and proceeded to patrol vacant lots, ditches, parks and creeks. I caught perch and a rockfish from Ambleside pier. A makeshift crab trap yielded a half-dozen crabs. My greens were young cattail heads, miner's lettuce, chicory, lamb's quarters, skunk cabbage, young dandelions and stinging nettles. Salmonberries, blackberries, huckleberries and thimbleberries completed the feast. With some trepidation, my sister and her friends sat down to sample my scavengings, attended by a photographer from *Weekend*. Apart from the skunk cabbage and stinging nettles (the sting is removed by boiling), the meal was declared a hit. And some weeks later a double full-page spread entitled "The Wild Banquet" appeared in *Weekend* with a photo of me resplendent in my sister's embroidered caftan. Ah, the things one does to get into print!

Sadly, the era of the Saturday supplement came to an abrupt end in the late '70s, but fortunately for me the adage, "When one door closes, another opens" has been true my whole life. A new magazine appeared about that time, aimed at the alternative-lifestyle, back-to-the-land folks. It was called *Harrowsmith* and was practically made for my talents. I became a regular contributor and wrote a piece about the decline of salmon stocks off the BC coast and another about a friend who had homesteaded on a remote island off the west coast of Vancouver Island, contrasting his lifestyle with mine in the interior of the province. I wrote about building my unique house and about my great friend Lloyd House (his real name), who designed it and helped me raise the main beams. (Lloyd's work as a designer and builder of alternative houses using local materials in the most ingenious ways is featured in *Builders of the Pacific Coast*, by Lloyd Kahn.)

Another time I wrote a story about a local "hippie fair" called the Barnes Creek Faire. I set the scene: it's a sizzling hot August day with (unusually) a police roadblock on the dusty road into the site, checking folks for drugs or other transgressions. The cops are sweating in their black uniforms, wishing they weren't here, and I watch them inspect the car in front of mine.

"Everybody out! Open the trunk!"

All the occupants oblige, including several little cherubs who giggle as they gambol around the cops.

"What the...? What about these kids?"

"Uh...what about them, officer? They're all ours..."

"They have no clothes on!"

You had to laugh. It's hard to make a case for public nudity against a three-year-old.

Harrowsmith published just about everything I sent in and paid well too. Then sometime in 1978, I wrote a piece on beer. It was titled "The Underground Brewmaster" and told people to start brewing their own beer, since not only was it much cheaper than the product from the liquor store (you avoided the compounded taxes, which at that time accounted for more than half the price), if you did it right, you could make a better, more satisfying drink than what the big guys produced. How to do it right was the gist of the article, coupled with some trenchant comments on how the mega brewing factories did it wrong. Here's an excerpt.

> The stage has been reached where all the big breweries are making virtually the same product, with different names and labels. Accompanying this trend is a shift in power from the hands of the brewmaster to the marketing, accounting and advertising men.
>
> Like tasteless white bread and the universal cardboard hamburger, the new beer is produced for the tasteless common denominator. It must not offend anyone, anywhere. Corporate beer is not too heavy, not too bitter, not too alcoholic, not too malty, not too hoppy, not too gassy or yeasty. In other words, corporate beer reduces every characteristic that makes beer beer.

The above has now been quoted so many times by beer writers in books and magazines that one author has termed it my "manifesto." Certainly at the time I didn't feel that I was writing anything earth-shaking. It was just an obvious comment from someone who had been "on the inside" of the Big Three. I didn't expect much of a reaction after the piece was published, and I didn't get any—for a long time. It took almost three years for the spark to find the right kindling.

In the summer of 1981, a few years after I had proudly moved into my new house, I got a phone call from a man with a very English accent. His name was John Mitchell, and he and two partners owned the Troller Pub in Horseshoe Bay, West Vancouver. He was fed up with the bland sameness of the Big Three beers on offer and he had an idea: why couldn't he brew and sell his own beers like the brewpubs he had known in England? His only problem was that he didn't know the first thing about brewing. When John had shared these thoughts over the bar with a friend, this fellow told him about an article he had read by an ex-employee of the big guys on how to make your own high-quality beer. The friend thought he still had the magazine and duly brought it in for John to read. That article was "The Underground Brewmaster."

"I read your article and was wondering if you could help me," John said on the phone. "I want to make a beautiful beer, a beer with character, like some you can still find in England. We've just been back there, and real ale is making a comeback, y'know."

After I got over my amusement at the enthusiasm of this guy who had *no* idea what he was getting into, I agreed to talk to him. But I wasn't going to Vancouver to do it. He would have to come to me. "It's a drive of 600 kilometres," I told him, thinking that would put him off.

But John was full of surprises. "No problem," he said. "I have the map of BC out and I can see where you are. Jenny and I have a week off. Should be there day after tomorrow."

And 48 hours later, here is this guy walking up to the house, bearing imported British beers and food to go with them. It was the start of a great association and friendship, though it had its amusing aspects. From the start I wondered how I, from my gritty working-class Manchester neighbourhood, would get along with this London-accented fellow from the upper middle class. When I had made them at home in my house (which they were most impressed with), John produced a bottle of beer made by an English craft brewery. It was dressed up in a fancy package, all British flags, crowns and stuff.

"For you," he said. "I brought two back from England. It's a commemoration special, but you have to drink it on Charlie's wedding day."

I was a little bemused. "Charlie who?" I asked.

"Why, Prince Charles, of course," John said with some astonishment. "He's getting married tomorrow!"

"Oh, *him*," I said. "I haven't thought about him in a decade or two. Not a big fan of the royals."

John and Jenny exchanged looks. "But you *do* have a television set?" asked Jenny hopefully. I told them I did, a little black-and-white model, rarely used. Reassured, they accepted my invitation to stay overnight, though it meant camping on the living room floor in their sleeping bags, the guest bedroom not having been built yet.

To the greeting party that evening I invited a couple, Chris and Susan, the only other Brits I knew of in our valley. We had a fine meal and lashings of good beer and wine—and I think a bottle of Scotch appeared later. I was more than tipsy when the evening ended. After Chris and Susan had gone and John and Jenny were preparing their sleeping bags in the living room, Jenny asked, "Is it all right if we turn on the TV in the morning? It starts at 5 a.m."

Oh, right, the bloody wedding! "You can turn it on," I said, "but if you wake me up, I'll show you the door." And I threw myself into bed.

The next morning I became conscious through a dull, painful fog. *Oh God, what had happened last night? Had I insulted my guests? Had they left?* I became aware of the sound of ethereal organ music. I thought, *Oh, right, I must be dead, and it's just like they said all along—it's going to be nothing but beautiful music and love, love, love from now on. The angels will be along in a minute.*

But the awful fog cleared after a while, and I gradually realized I had not achieved my apotheosis but was lying in my bed with a prizewinning hangover. Still the beautiful music continued, though very faint. I crawled out of bed and peeped around the door. There were John and Jenny, sitting up in their sleeping bags, sipping tea and watching Charles and Diana coming down the aisle to a wonderful, gentle organ passage.

"Good morning!" they said. "Like some tea?"

It was July 29, 1981. I groaned and went back to bed.

After this inauspicious start, we got down to business. What was it that John really wanted from me? He explained that he had been trained as a chef at London's Westminster Technical Institute. After he came to Canada, he worked at the Banff Springs Hotel, then behind the bar at the Vancouver Club and for fifteen years at the Sylvia Hotel before buying into the Troller Pub. They'd just returned from a trip to England, and he showed me a pile of pamphlets and newsletters from the Campaign for Real Ale (CAMRA). "Why can't we do this here?" he asked. "Why not?" I replied and assured him that I could design a small brewing plant for him within his budget and even formulate recipes to suit the "real ale" style he was after.

"What do you want it to taste like?" I asked.

"Fuller's London Pride," said John.

"Right. Then get hold of some bottles of it and I'll figure out the recipe."

But I told him there was no point in going ahead with the nuts and bolts of a brewery for his pub until he had a licence for it, which was a major undertaking since no such licence existed within BC's liquor laws. And from my experience I knew that BC's Liquor Control Board (LCB) did not move fast on any new proposals—if it moved at all. In addition, things might get hung up with federal law. I told John he needed a carefully worded proposal to present to the LCB outlining what we had in mind.

"Where would I get that? Lawyers?" asked John.

I shook my head. "I can do it right here. I've been writing professionally for nine years and know the beer business and the LCB as well as anyone. Why don't you and Jenny go off and explore the Kootenays for four days? That will give me time to think, and when you come back, I hope to have prepared a proposal that you can present to them."

"You think you can do it?" John seemed doubtful.

"Well," I said, "you'll find out when you come back."

So off they went, and I started work on the proposal.

When they returned, I was hoeing weeds in my garden. John and Jenny sat and watched for a while, the burning question hovering in the air. I'm sure they were still wondering about this somewhat odd individual with his longish hair and beard and his sandals, happily hoeing his beans. Could he really do what he said he could?

"So, how did you get on?" asked John tentatively.

"Oh, it's all done," I replied. "Ready for you to take back to town. A first draft, for sure. It may need alterations and additions when you go over it with your partners, lawyers and so forth, but it's all in there, written in a way that should appeal to the LCB. Good luck with it, but don't be surprised if you don't hear back from them this year. And don't be surprised if their answer is no."

They came up to the house, and we went over the proposal. John was impressed. This curious chap was indeed *just* the man he needed to bring his idea to fruition! Off they went back to Vancouver the next day, proposal in hand, brimming with new hope, despite my warnings about the pitfalls of dealing with the LCB and an inert government. I didn't expect my phone to ring anytime soon.

7 We Get Our Licence and Bay Ale Is Born

WHAT IF BACK IN THE SUMMER OF '81 THAT GUY IN THE pub hadn't dug out that copy of *Harrowsmith* with "The Underground Brewmaster" in it for John Mitchell? What if I had never written it or John had not pursued the idea? Coincidences? Or were the stars aligned just right for us? As our unlikely journey toward a brewing licence proceeded, I was inclined to believe the latter.

Interesting things were happening at the old Liquor Control Board that had nothing whatsoever to do with our application. From 1951 to 1969 the LCB, which was supposedly a three-member board, had been under the total control of one man, its chairman, Colonel Donald McGugan. His position as czar was safe under Premier W.A.C. Bennett's Social Credit government because Bennett was a non-drinker, and the two men shared a determination to keep tight control over this potentially dangerous stuff called alcohol. (Roy Peterson, cartoonist for the *Vancouver Sun*, used to portray "Wacky" Bennett and his Socred bigwigs wearing big floppy hats with large circular crowns. When asked why he'd chosen the peculiar headgear, he replied, "It's to hide their halos!") The incorruptible and autocratic McGugan's decisions on licensing had no right of appeal and were never explained. He even refused to give licences to establishments that had been approved by the government. Finally he became such an embarrassment that the government pre-emptively announced his "retirement" in 1969, when he was just shy of his eightieth birthday.

However, it took until 1973 and a change of government to the New Democratic Party before significant changes to the liquor laws were allowed, including the licensing of neighbourhood pubs such as John Mitchell's Troller Pub as an alternative to the soulless, barn-like, male-dominated "beer parlours." Fortunately, even when the Socreds came back into power under W.A.C.'s son, Bill Bennett Jr., in 1975, there was no return to the bad old days. In fact, Bennett Jr., a drinker, instituted even more changes in the miserly liquor laws. The old LCB became the Liquor Control and Licensing Branch (LCLB) and was placed under the Ministry of Consumer and Corporate Affairs, a portfolio that in 1981 went to a bright new lawyer, Peter Hyndman, who promptly announced that the government was unhappy with the lack of price competition in the beer marketplace. The government would therefore stop setting the price of beer, leaving the breweries to set their own prices. It now seems unbelievable, but up to that point the government had set the price of beer, and all beers were priced the same! (Well, of course, they all *tasted* the same...)

About this time John Mitchell had a meeting with Allan Gould, general manager of the LCLB, and was apparently told, "I've been sitting here thinking why your idea can't work, and I haven't come up with anything." Still, Gould explained, the person John had to convince was Hyndman. So John took our proposal to the Ministry of Consumer and Corporate Affairs, where it was given the "hot potato" treatment as it was tossed from one bureaucrat to the next, no one knowing what to do with it. And each time he showed up at the LCLB offices in Vancouver to ask about progress, he was told, "Ah yes, we're studying it, Mr. Mitchell."

Six months went by after Hyndman deregulated the price of beer with nothing happening on the beer pricing front. Then within three weeks of each other, the Big Three raised their prices by the same amount. The press had a field day. So this was price competition as practised by the big boys? No collusion here? Hyndman was naturally embarrassed, and he called a meeting with the Big Three bosses.

Covering the story for the *Vancouver Sun* was business reporter Der Hoi-Yin. She was waiting outside Hyndman's office when the meeting broke up, and the Big Three boys filed past her with "no comment, no comment and no comment." When Hyndman appeared, she asked him what had gone on in there.

"Well," he said, "I told them that I was most unhappy with their response to the expected pricing differences, and if they couldn't do better, they may find themselves getting competition from elsewhere."

"But where?" she asked. It was a good question, since the Big Three were the only players in this poker game.

"Well," he said, "we've been thinking of introducing American beer again." (It had been brought in during the strike/lockout at the Big Three breweries in the summer of 1978.) "And," he added, "there is a group who own a pub in

West Vancouver who want to brew their own beer to sell in the pub, and we are seriously considering their application."

A pub making its own unique beer? Unheard of! When the story hit the paper, it was not so much about the big guys but about this radical new concept, the pub brewery that was about to be launched in Horseshoe Bay. We were about to be used as a tiny stick to beat the big boys—I loved it. The next time John went to the LCLB offices, his reception was completely different.

"So, gentlemen, I hear we're getting our licence?"

"Apparently so, Mr. Mitchell. But you'll have to go to Victoria and discuss your plans with the minister."

Then my phone was ringing and John was saying, "Appleton! You better get yourself ready. Things are really starting to move around here."

When he told me what had happened, I shook my head in disbelief. "Look out for a building near the pub for the brewery," I told him. "About a thousand square feet should do it." John told me he already had his eye on an empty boat shop at Sewell's Marina. When could I come down to have a look at it? His excitement was palpable.

The unit John had found in the marina was a diminutive 770 square feet—basically one large ground-floor room. Space would be tight, but it would serve. We could save some space by putting the malt mill and auger on a dolly so they could be wheeled out of the way. To save money, we bought a used dairy batch pasteurizer vessel for the mash tun, and in the UK we found a source of used eight-hundred-litre, stainless-steel, pressure-rated vessels to use as our storage tanks. John had moved a drafting board into his spare bedroom for me, and on this I drew up the floor plan and the designs for the brew kettle and two open fermenters, and we had them fabricated locally. Then John and I added insulation and cedar cladding to the kettle. John insisted on a red tile floor. It was a cute little brewery and seemed quite charming to me, since I'd only worked in mega factories. We spent a total of about $35,000 on equipment, and the total spent on the entire brewery about $70,000, most of it on building modifications.

The result was about as simple as you can make a brewing plant. The kettle—one large stainless pot with a gas burner under it—was used to preheat the brewing water to "mashing in" temperature and later to bring the wort (the liquid extract from the mash) to a boil. The mash was made in the mash tun by mixing ground barley malt with the heated water (using a canoe paddle) and allowing it to sit for 90 minutes while the diastase enzymes inherent in the malt converted the starch into sugars (infusion mash). After that, the "sweet wort" was drawn off the mash and pumped to the kettle, where it was brought to a boil; hops were added in stages throughout the 90-minute boil. The wort was then cooled by pumping it through a tiny plate heat-exchanger that we got from New Zealand before running it to one of the fermenters. Yeast was added, and fermentation took place over about a week. Then the beer was pumped to a storage tank in our tiny cold room, where we added finings, better known as isinglass, a gelatinous colloid used to help clarify the beer. It was an article of faith with John and me *not* to filter our beer to get rid of unwanted sediment, as too much filtration removes proteins that are flavour components. Besides, we wanted a fraction of active yeast left to produce a secondary fermentation after the beer was run into the kegs, making it "tight" with CO_2 for serving. The whole process took three to four weeks. Cask-conditioned beer! Live beer! Just like they used to make.

There were some things we couldn't save money on, like the barley malt we used. The complexities of the malting process are such that, when I was studying malting and brewing science in college, it seemed beyond belief to me that ancient humankind had stumbled on the process of turning grain into something that produced sugars, which could then be fermented to make an alcoholic drink. If you make a mash of dried mature grain in water, it does nothing. You can cook it and make a porridge or gruel that's edible, but it's not sweet and it won't ferment. The only things available to ancient people that would naturally ferment were fruits containing sugars, but in northern Europe the only things people could make something alcoholic from was a mash of apples, pears or berries, but it was weak stuff and often sour since the sugar content was so low. In the sunny countries to the south, grapes could be grown with a sugar content of 20 percent or higher, so they made wine and transported it long distances to more northern regions, where it commanded very high prices. That left the common people of those northern countries, who couldn't afford imported wine, to create an affordable beverage from what was available—grain, which those northern regions had plenty of.

But how do you make something fermentable from tough barley grains? You do it via the malting process, first wetting the grain so it will start to sprout. The first signs of this are a rosette of tiny rootlets that emerge from the bottom of the seed. The shoot, or acrospire, that will become the stem of the plant also starts to grow, but at first you can't see it, since it grows beneath the outer husk of the seed. Just as this "chit" starts to emerge, you terminate the process by drying it. What has happened? The seed has produced the diastatic enzymes necessary to turn the starch in the seed into sugars for plant growth. If you don't heat it too much when drying, the enzymes are retained in the dried seed, and if later you grind it and make a mash of it in warm water, the enzymes are reactivated and will convert the rest of the starch into sugars.

Sound simple? It isn't. Once germination starts, you must turn the grain bed frequently or the rootlets will quickly form a tangled mass that will be impossible to turn. An unturned grain bed that isn't aerated will quickly sour and yield a smelly mess that is useless. Then there's the drying process. Too hot and the enzymes are destroyed. Too cool and mould plus smelly, slimy bacteria take over and ruin the batch. The grain bed must also be constantly turned during the drying process. Control of temperature and humidity must be precise for success in malting. How did primitive human beings ever manage it? Or even discover it?

I pondered these questions for a long time. Then it dawned on me. Consider this: you have succeeded in growing a fine crop of barley (or other grain) on the land around your primitive village. You make it into sheaves and stack them up to dry in the fields. Then a torrential rainstorm hits. The grain gets drenched. It's a disaster. You have to do something—this is your winter's food supply, and left in the field, it will sprout in the sheaf and go mouldy. In desperation you drag the sheaves under cover and build a fire to dry them, turning them to expose them to the heat, and somehow you manage to get them dry before they go mouldy. Then later you make that salvaged grain into bread or gruel. It tastes good—slightly sweet and definitely better than the original grain. You don't know why this is the case, but slowly you get the idea that wet grain soon dried will produce this magical effect every time, and if you decant the sweet liquor from the gruel you make from it, then add the mysterious stuff that makes bread rise, you will have a frothy alcoholic drink. These beer beginnings must have seen a multitude of spoiled batches of sprouted grains and gruel liquor, but slowly, slowly people learned how to eliminate the bad batches and without understanding why, malting was achieved.

In 1982, when John Mitchell and I set out to brew our first ale, there was just one giant malting plant in the western half of the country, Canada Malting in Calgary, which was largely owned by the Big Three brewers, for whom it cranked out tens of thousands of tons of one product: pale lager malt suitable for adjunct lager beers. I knew this wouldn't work for us. What we needed was English-style malt made from two-row barley strains like Maris Otter, Golden Promise or Ark Royal, all of them highly modified malts with *low* protein and high starch content. The big brewers often used six-row malts, which have relatively high levels of protein but yield less fermentable extract. Why would you use something that gave *less* extract? Well, six-row types have a higher diastatic power (DP), which is the measure of the enzymes needed to convert the starch into sugars. Remember that 40 to 50 percent cornstarch "adjunct" used in domestic lagers by the Big Three? It has no diastase itself, and the brewers rely on the enzymes provided by the barley malt to convert this straight starch to sugars. But as the percentage of adjunct creeps higher, a point is reached (above 50 percent) where the malt enzymes cannot convert all this extra starch. The solution? Not to cut back on the adjunct, but to introduce some six-row malt, which has a higher DP than two-row. After I explained the situation to John, he didn't hesitate. "Right!" he said. "We'll bring in our malt from England!" And we did, in twenty-foot container loads.

Curiously, after Bay Ale had been on tap for some months, I got a letter from Canada Malting saying it had come to their attention that we were importing English malt for our beer. This was just not on, they said, as Canadian beer should be made from Canadian malt, and they hinted that it might even be against trade laws to make and sell beer in Canada made from imported malt. I replied that we would be only too happy to buy their malt if they could provide highly modified two-row strains like Maris Otter that were suitable for ales with protein levels less than 10 percent. I never got a reply. It is gratifying to see that in the past few years Canada Malting has got the idea that there is indeed a market out there for malt types other than pale lager malt, and it is now producing a line of malts suitable for craft brewers. A sign of the times.

*

The yeast for our ale was another crucial issue, just as it had been for the ancients. Having solved the malting process, they must have discovered quite accidentally that if you added some of the mysterious beige frothy goop that made bread rise to the sweet liquor decanted from your gruel, it would make a frothy alcoholic drink. What was this goop? Nobody knew. It was termed the "good rot" or "God rot" to distinguish it from all the bad rots that ruined food and drink. The people of northern Europe called it *gischt* or *gyst*, which means "foam," and that became "yeast" in England, or more commonly "barm." All they knew was that, as it interacted with the liquor from the gruel, it formed a froth on the surface (or lay on the bottom when the liquid was removed), and if they collected it and added it to a new batch of gruel liquor, it would start a ferment. The process was thought to be an act of "spontaneous generation" or abiogenesis, which was the popular theory that, if left to itself, decaying organic matter would produce primitive life forms. Almighty God did it. How else to explain that the finest, unique beers in northern Europe were made by monks in monasteries? It had to be because they were praying all the time! Of course, it was more likely to be because the monks were scrupulously careful in their methods and wrote them down so the next generation could follow them.

We've been using yeast for thousands of years. Where did the early people get it? The winemakers among them had it easy. The pale white "bloom" that you can rub off the skin of the grape turns out to be airborne yeasts that are trying to get at the sugars in the grapes. Crush the ripe grapes, and *voila*! You have a fermentation. The beer makers had a more difficult time procuring yeast and mostly relied on the "sour dough" from bread making. But if you take any sweet fruit, crush it in water and leave it out in the air in warm weather, nine times out of ten it will start to ferment from airborne organisms infecting it. Whether those organisms produce the kind of alcoholic fermentation you want is a gamble at this point, so you do a bit of quality control—you taste it. Tastes bad? Throw it out and try again. Tastes good? Use it to start the next batch. If that turns out good as well, you save the foamy stuff to inoculate the next batch, and so on. You keep throwing out the bad batches and saving the good, plus retrieving the barm from the good. What you are doing is selecting for and propagating the stuff that will do the job right.

In the 1670s, when Anton van Leeuwenhoek built the first primitive microscopes, he described a whole world of tiny "animalcules" he had found in pond water and other liquids. He also saw minute globular particles in beer (yeast cells) but did not think them living creatures since they did not move, unlike most of his tiny animals. In the 1830s de la Tour, Schwann and Kutzing proved that yeast was the cause of fermentation and suggested it was a tiny vegetable organism. Three decades later, further refinement of the microscope enabled Louis Pasteur to note that yeast was a single-celled micro-organism. His groundbreaking discoveries were funded by the French breweries and wineries, which wanted to know why some batches went sour, and Pasteur was able to demonstrate that it was due to the growth of other organisms than yeast in the liquid. He showed them that it was possible to kill those organisms by heating the grape juice or wort to 140°F for twenty minutes—"pasteurization"—then cooling it. Introduce a fresh strain of yeast, and no more spoiled batches. No more mystery. It was the beginning of applied microbiology.

At the time it was thought that these tiny organisms must be related to the even tinier organisms that Robert Koch had described when he peered into improved microscopes that could magnify five hundred times to examine the body fluids of anthrax victims. He called them "bakteria" from the Greek meaning "little sticks." Later the assumption that yeast cells and bacteria were related was shown not to be the case; instead, yeast cells are actually single-celled forms of fungi that do not (usually) form spores but reproduce by simple division of the cell (budding). They are called *fungi imperfecti*, or "imperfect fungus." It is a sobering thought that yeast cells are closer to ourselves genetically than to bacteria. The main problem in brewery fermentations, even today, is making sure that when you add yeast from a previous batch, you are not adding spoilage organisms along with the yeast.

But beer makers found another trick to success. We now know that alcoholic fermentation is an anaerobic process, that is, it happens in the absence of air. But *Saccharomyces*, the sugar-loving fungus, needs oxygen for growth. How to cater to this problem? It turns out not to be too difficult: if you aerate the wort slightly by whipping some surface air into it when adding the yeast, the cells will happily reproduce by the millions. Once they are started, you deny oxygen to the batch, and the alcoholic fermentation proceeds until all the available sugar is turned into alcohol and CO_2. Of course, these days, because we are so afraid of airborne contaminants, when we add the yeast, we inject sterile air or bottled oxygen for this purpose.

For John and I the big question was: Where do we get a pure strain of yeast that is identical to the yeast that was used to ferment ales a hundred years ago in England? In 1982 there were no private labs like Wyeast or White Labs, which are now able to provide a wide range of pure yeast strains in convenient one-litre liquid cultures, ready to be pitched into a brew. So who would we order our yeast from? The answer was the National Collection of Yeast Cultures (NCYC) in England. The NCYC is the microbiologist's reference library, a collection of micro-organisms that have been important to humankind in the last century. They lie dormant there in tiny hermetically sealed and freeze-dried culture tubes. There are literally hundreds of listings for *Saccharomyces cerevisiae* (sugar-loving beer yeast) in the NCYC catalogue to choose from, but fortunately a chart is provided. These days you can get a computer printout giving enough biochemical information on the metabolism of these tiny phenomenal producers of alcohol to drive you to drink. But in 1982, like the brewers of old, I looked specifically at five things on the chart: yeast deposited at the top, yeast deposited at the bottom, rate of fermentation, degree of attenuation (how far fermentation goes before it stops) and clarity after fermentation.

What we wanted was a true top-fermenting yeast. Traditional ale yeast forms gelatinous flocs, which clump together and rise to the surface of the beer, borne by CO_2 bubbles, to form a thick, sticky layer. Lager yeast does not form flocs but instead breaks into tiny aggregates or separate cells, which sink to the bottom of the fermenter when spent. Ale yeast has the advantage of providing protection from aerial contamination in open-top fermenters with its thick coating, but it requires regular skimming. This leaves the fermented beer clearer than lager yeast, which tends to hang around, trying to ferment the last bits of complex sugars. So with these considerations in mind, I pored over the scores of ale yeasts in the NCYC catalogue, narrowing it down to a half-dozen, which I pointed out to John. One of them was NCYC 1313.

"Are you superstitious?" I asked him.

"Thirteen is my lucky number!" he said. "And two thirteens must be doubly lucky. Let's get that one."

So we did, though I did order some of the others to hedge our bets. In the end 1313 was what we used.

When our yeast arrived, a tiny bit of dry, brown residue at the bottom of a sealed vial the size of a child's pinky, John looked dubious. Fortunately he had an in-house microbiologist who knew how to coax this speck of inert cells back to life. I had brought some culture tubes, pipettes and culture media from home, and we turned John and Jenny's kitchen into a makeshift lab, swabbing the countertops with alcohol and sterilizing all our equipment in the pressure cooker. Any contamination at this stage would have meant disaster. Then carefully opening the vial, I introduced a millilitre of liquid medium, flicked the tube to dissolve the yeast residue, then sucked the contents out with the same pipette, transferring this to a ten-millilitre culture tube containing liquid yeast extract medium. Then, along with other prepared tubes, the yeast was incubated in a nice, warm spot over the water heater. It takes time for freeze-dried cells to wake up, but when I saw some turbidity in the tubes after a week, it put a smile on my face. Now all we had to do was keep expanding the culture every few days until we had twenty litres of actively fermenting wort—enough "starter" for a full brew. A fermenting agent that might have been the closely kept secret of a brewery a hundred years ago was about to be the yeast that would produce the first craft beer in Canada.

Many things have been used to flavour and preserve fermented drinks from spoilage over the centuries. Among them are spruce needles, heather, bog myrtle, yarrow, wild rosemary, juniper berries, ginger, caraway seed, aniseed, nutmeg and cinnamon, sometimes in combinations that were carefully guarded secrets. These mixtures were called gruit, and the beverage obtained was called gruit ale. By the fourteenth century, hops were being grown and used for flavouring ale in the Netherlands, but their use was vigorously resisted in other parts of Europe by the established gruit makers—mainly the monasteries—because it had long been known that hops had a mildly soporific effect. In fact, soft hop cones were used to make "hop pillows" to induce sleep. When England was at war with the Netherlands in the 1600s, adulterating gruit ale with hops was thought to be a nasty Dutch plot to put the honest English yeomen to sleep while the Dutch invaded, and growing or using hops was banned by royal edict. It is also interesting that hops, *Humulus lupulus*, is included in the genus *Cannabaceae*, which also contains cannabis. Both are prized for the resins produced in their buds, but hop oils don't produce similar effects to cannabis. (I know because I've tried them.)

However, the bitter flavour of hopped beer gradually gained more adherents in Europe, and in spite of the initial resistance, within two hundred years of their introduction, hops had replaced gruit in almost all the beer produced there. And there was more to it: hop oils have an antiseptic quality that suppresses beer spoilage bacteria, and thus they act as a preservative. These oils also reduce the surface tension of the wort, giving a more even, controlled boil, and they promote the precipitation of soluble proteins and tannins to insoluble "trub," which is the name for the solids left in the liquid after the boil. Beers made without hops are stubbornly cloudy. For these reasons, hops and hop flavours are now indispensable to beer making. The English types of hops were easiest for John and I to obtain because, thanks to plant breeding programs in Washington state and Oregon, most of the classic European hops were being grown in areas around Yakima and in the Willamette

Valley. John and I settled for the old English types, Fuggles and Kent Goldings, which were readily available and gave a milder, traditional English hop flavour. Today cross-bred hybrids and cloning have produced entirely new varieties, and the brewer has a whole new range of hops to choose from, varieties that did not even exist when I was studying brewing.

Meanwhile, we brought in small amounts of English malts and hops and prepared test batches from the recipe I had formulated as our version of London Pride. It was to be called Bay Ale. The results were encouraging—though they would not be exactly the same as the finished product. They never are.

*

All this time I had been living with the Mitchells at their home, which was situated in a wonderful spot in Copper Cove with an incredible view of Howe Sound. From there I went for walks over a rocky bluff and into Whytecliff Park, where the eagles wheeled overhead and curious seals looked me in the eye. But I was more interested in the beautiful rock-paved walkway around the Mitchells' house, as well as the rock walls and garden shed and barbecue pit. The source of the rock was evident: the house stood in front of a huge cliff, which over the centuries had shed slabs of granite into what was now the Mitchells' backyard. In this aspect it had a lot in common with my own place, which had been built using trees cleared to make room for it.

"Who did all this rock work?" I asked. John confessed that he had done it and explained, "There were a few Italian stonemasons working around here, and I learned from them." This was a revelation: he had done something that I had been dreaming about, building useful and beautiful things from rock that most people would consider an impediment. No wonder he had been so enthusiastic about my place in the Kootenays. Over the years that followed our brewery project, John would think nothing of making the long drive to my place, rolling up his sleeves and sharing the rock splitting and building techniques he had learned. We had a wonderful working relationship: I taught him brewing, and he taught me stonemasonry. What a guy!

But with our very different backgrounds we did have some comical differences. One morning in June 1982 I emerged from my bedroom at his house to find John breakfasting in the kitchen with his eyes glued to a TV set. On the screen, armoured troops were being unloaded from planes and helicopters and advancing over something that looked like the Yorkshire moors. Were those British flags?

"We've taken Port Stanley!" said John, pleased.

"What?" My newly awakened brain cells focused on reality. Oh no! The Falklands War!

"We've taken Port Stanley," said John again, "and the Argies are packing up!"

I was dismayed. "John! This is the last gasp of a faded empire! It's a billion-dollar 'rally round the flag' use of taxpayers' money to get Maggie Thatcher elected again!"

"Harruumph!" was John's only comment.

"I don't know about you, but I'm a Canadian..." I said.

"Well, *I'm* a Canadian too," he countered.

"Well then, what do you mean by *we've* taken Port Stanley?"

By May 1982 all the elements of the brewery were in place. Drains had been inserted into the floors and the floors tiled, the water supply upgraded, natural gas and electrical systems installed, the walls painted white, all the vessels placed and connected, and a giant plate glass window put in to show off our little pride and joy—the Horseshoe Bay Brewery. Despite its diminutive size and out-of-the-way location, it attracted a lot of attention. It was, after all, the first craft brewery—or "cottage brewery"—in Canada and, I believe, in North America. (The word *brewpub* came later when a change in federal licensing laws allowed pubs to brew *and* sell their products on the same premises.)

The moment finally came to move the sixteen kegs from our first batch, which had been filled; "primed" with a tiny amount of yeast, dextrose and isinglass; then bunged and left in the warm brewhouse to secondary-ferment for a week. We loaded them gently—"like unexploded bombs," as John put it—into John's truck and drove them the short distance to the pub. There we put them into the pub cooler and left them to settle.

Thursday, June 17, 1982, was the big day. There was an expectant crowd in the pub, but John and I were back in the cellar, secretly tapping the first keg. When I looked at the first glass, my heart fell: it wasn't clear. And it was a bit on the "flat" side. Maybe the finings hadn't worked in taking the yeast down? Then I realized that the haze wasn't yeast, it was chill haze. The soluble protein from all that lovely English malt we'd used had come out of solution when subjected to the frigid temperatures in the Troller Pub's cooler, which had been set at 3°C to cater to the domestic lagers. And the coldness had made our English-style low carbonation seem flat. We needed to serve our beer a few degrees warmer. Suddenly we had another problem to overcome—we really needed two coolers set at different temperatures if we wanted to serve both "real ale" and domestic lagers. And to be "really real," the ale had to be served via hand pumps, not pushed through draft towers with CO_2 pressure. John looked crestfallen. But the flavour of the beer was excellent, and as I realized what the problem was, I devised a plan. "We're going to have to wait," I told him. "We need to turn up the temperature in this cooler and increase the CO_2 top pressure to give it a bit more fizz, and I think it'll come right by tomorrow. Let's go and have some supper." And we did.

But by 9 p.m. John couldn't contain himself any longer. "Let's go down to the pub and see how the beer's getting on." So off we went. When we drew a pint this time, the beer foamed up to make a nice head, and though not perfectly clear, it was definitely improved. John sampled the pint and a big grin spread across his face. He threw his arms around me. "You've done it, my boy! You've done it!" And we did a little jig around the cellar. "Let's put it on tap right now and see how it goes."

The hype preceding our launch meant there was a full house of thirsty beer buffs, currently drinking Carling's Pilsener. John ran off a glass and handed it to the nearest customer. "Taste that!" he said. "That is the first 'real ale' to be produced in Canada in modern times!" He gave away glass after glass, and the bar was jammed. Soon the whole pub was joyously quaffing pints of the stuff. The haze disappeared as the beer warmed.

The beer disappeared fast too. In the days that followed, Bay Ale outsold the domestic lagers two to one. John had thought we would have to sell at least two kegs a day to break even. The first full day, we sold six and rapidly realized we would have to limit the pub to four kegs a day so as not to run out of beer all the time. It was a hit! We were in all the newspapers and got a flood of free publicity.

After a month or so of steady production, an improving product, and the installation of a young brewer trained by John, it was time for me to head back to the Kootenays. John and I had fulfilled his dream of brewing just the style of beer he wanted and selling it to enthusiastic patrons in his pub. My feeling was that it would be a small, local success that would keep him occupied for many happy years. I didn't expect that within two years he would be involved in building a brand-new brewpub in Victoria, nor did I anticipate that I would be kept busy for the next twenty years designing and bringing on-stream brewpubs and micro-breweries in Canada, the US and France.

8 A Tale of Two Cities' Brewpubs

HERE'S AN INTERESTING PUZZLE: TWO IDENTICAL, SHINY new brewing plants made by the same manufacturer with the same brewing consultant (me) are brought on-stream at the same time (1984). One is in Victoria, the other in Winnipeg. One becomes a great success, the other a dismal failure. Why?

The old saying about "location, location, location" being the three most important words when starting a business could not have been truer than in this case. Spinnakers, now iconic, was purpose-built from the ground up, a beautiful building on an outstanding site overlooking the entrance to Victoria's Inner Harbour. It was also in the "very tweedy" capital of BC, which boasted the most ex-patriate Brits in the country, eager for a pint that reminded them of home. Friday's Bar, in contrast, was shoehorned into a Travelodge Hotel on the outskirts of Winnipeg. Its clientele during the day was the typical baseball-hatted, middle-aged "beer parlour crowd," and in the evening after the mandatory dinner-hour closure, it reinvented itself as a disco bar.

Spinnakers had John Mitchell who, after winning accolades for starting his own brewery in Horseshoe Bay, the first in Canada, had been tempted by the offer of partnership in the Spinnakers project. It was a chance he couldn't pass up, a chance to build a brewpub *exactly* as he wanted, with more space, a grain loft over the brewhouse, beer coolers at different temperatures for the ales and lagers, and English hand pumps for the real ales—all the little details that we hadn't been able to accommodate at the Troller. It was the perfect brewpub.

Friday's Bar didn't have someone like John to chase the details, so they hired me—though unfortunately not until the brewing plant was about to be installed. The floor plan had already been decided and major oversights already incorporated: no filters for product water, floor drains in the wrong place (or none at all) and no air conditioning in the brewhouse. The cellar was an awkward distance from the brewhouse, so that we had to use walkie-talkies when running transfers from fermentation to storage. The owner of the hotel, Colin Noble, was from Northern Ireland, where he had other hotels, so he was absent from Winnipeg for long periods of time, making it difficult to get decisions made. When I arrived on the scene, no attempt had been made to vet likely candidates for brewer, and the one I was offered was Peter Wong, a cook from the hotel kitchen who had emigrated from Brunei. He had no experience with brewing and no idea what real ale was supposed to taste like.

The start-up of the Spinnakers plant (for which John had hired me) went pretty smoothly; that of Friday's Bar was fraught with problems. John had worked as a chef in high-end restaurants and behind the bar in the best clubs in Vancouver before buying into the Troller Pub. He loved good food and drink, and loved serving it up for others. He was *the* hotelier *par excellence*, the publican you want to see behind the bar—cheerful, friendly, totally involved with the customers and the fine fare he was providing. Colin Noble was a hotel owner who had business interests on both sides of the Atlantic, not a hands-on person at all. He was ambitious—maybe too ambitious in this case. Before his brewing plant was even installed, let alone making good-quality beer, he had created Nobleman Brewing Ltd. and signed an agreement with SPR, the England-based makers of the plant, giving Nobleman the exclusive rights to market and sell SPR equipment in North America. He had even hired a salesman, when we didn't have a competent brewer for his showpiece brewery. The illustrated pamphlets he had printed up advertised the capabilities of Nobleman, and I found myself featured as "Frank Appleton, one of North America's most knowledgeable brewing consultants, heads up the technical side of Nobleman Brewing Ltd." as if there were a squad of technicians behind me waiting to get to work. Of course, there was nobody, and I had not agreed to lend my reputation to help sell Nobleman's brewing plants. The only pay I received was for my time in getting the Winnipeg plant up and running, and as soon as it was, though it was still struggling against the difficulties caused by the lack of foresight in the planning, I was glad to get on a plane to Victoria and go work with the competent and sensible John Mitchell.

But it wasn't long before I got panicked calls from Peter and had to head back to Winnipeg. Poor Peter! He was really out of his depth. Not only did he have no brewing background or even knowledge of what beer in process should taste like, his language difficulties kept him from talking to customers about the pub's beers and why they were superior to the mainstream lagers. And there were endless equipment problems: the screen in the hop back that strained the spent hops was too flimsy and it buckled, allowing hop particles to get by and plug up the plate heat-exchanger used to cool the wort. As a result, we had to dismantle the unit every brew, adding an hour to our day. The fridge plant that cooled the water circulated through the fermenter jackets and heat-exchanger was inadequate for the task. As we started into summer, the temperature in the brewhouse whenever we were brewing rapidly rose above 30°C. There was no air conditioning in there, just an extraction fan, but as nobody had thought to provide a cold-air inlet for makeup air, this was ineffective. The fridge plant worked overtime trying to keep the brews down at 20°C when the temperature outside the fermenters was 35°C, so it wasn't long before the motor burned out. We had problems getting parts from England. And then there were issues with the quality of the city water supply, which in the heat of the Manitoba summer seriously declined with a lot of dead algae and other organics in it. The city dealt with the problem by raising the chlorine level. All of this was anathema to good brewing water, and I spent some time searching out the right sediment and activated-carbon filters and getting them installed.

Another thing that bothered both Peter and me was being on display every minute of our brewing day, which was unavoidable because the brewing plant had been laid out behind a wall of plate glass along one side of the barroom. Now, I am fully in favour of showing your brewing plant off if it is well made and attractive. Brewing plants are fine examples of industrial art and people like to look at them, but to put your brewers in a goldfish bowl setting where their every move is watched by a slightly inebriated bar crowd is somewhat unnerving. It is quite normal in a brewery for tank lees to be run onto the floor and hosed down the drain, but this event would be greeted by shouts and laughter from the pub: "Hey, the Chinese guy's flushing the brew down the drain!" and other such mindless banter. No wonder Peter felt uncomfortable. Put your brewery on show by all means, but do it so that the public can see the brewery from *outside* the pub, and the brewer can go about his or her job without constant scrutiny from the bar.

But perhaps the worst thing about the crowd that frequented Friday's Bar was that they didn't even like our beer! There were no expat Brits, as in Victoria, thirsting for a good old pint. These were solid, stolid, Canadian lager drinkers. Even after we had struggled through all the problems and finally come up with a decent "real ale," the local pub crowd found it too heavy or too hoppy or a bit flat, or they made some other derisive comment before going back to their adjunct lager. That was the daytime bar crowd. After the mandatory dinner-hour closing, the bar opened again as a disco joint with deafening music and patrons barely out of their teens. They were more into wine coolers and light beers; real ale wasn't even on their radar. "We have to make a light lager like the big boys," said Colin Noble. This capitulation made me cringe, not only because fighting the mega brewers' flavourless fizz was what the Real Ale Movement was all about, but also because SPR's brewing plant was not set up for lager production, and I knew we couldn't make a success of it. We tried but failed. The young crowd went back to their light beers and coolers.

Winnipeg was a tough crowd to win over, and it's still like that. In fact, the Prairies in general are a desert when it comes to real ale.

Flying back to Victoria, the contrast was like coming out of the night and into daylight. Spinnakers was packed with happy folks enjoying a choice of fine ales and some of the best pub food you could find. In any well-run brew-pub, the food generates 50 percent of the revenue, drink the other half. Nobody went to Friday's Bar for the food. True, you could order food from the hotel kitchen but it was nothing special, and besides, the ambience of the bar was inimical to sitting down to a meal with friends. It still felt like one of the old "beer parlours." In Victoria, John had designed and oversaw not only the brewery but the kitchen too, and the food was superlative—way beyond what you normally find as "pub food." The oysters Rockefeller were the best I had ever tasted, and the rest of the menu was equally creative and delicious. People came for the food as much as the beer.

The success of Spinnakers was such that management was faced with the ridiculous situation of having to hire someone to be on the door to regulate the lineup and *keep out* trade because, as a neighbourhood pub, it was restricted to a mere 65 seats plus 10 percent standing. But even with a popular, successful operation, it was hard to make money with only 65 seats. When the pub legislation was drafted by the NDP, there had been provision for 100-seat licences as well as 65-seaters, but after the Social Credit government came to power again, the LCLB stopped granting new 100-seat licences. This was, no doubt, due to pressure from the BC Hotel Association, whose characterless beer parlours had the vast majority of the draft beer trade; they weren't about to give any of it up. Spinnakers had been approved by the fire marshal for 120 seats, and all John wanted was one of the old 100-seat licences so that he could let in the people clamouring for a seat and start to make some money on his investment. When the government wouldn't budge, John started to let in a few more people. But suddenly anonymous inspectors from the liquor board began showing up and surreptitiously counting heads, and John was notified that if he didn't keep his patrons down to 65, his licence would be suspended. Who had tipped the LCLB off that John was exceeding his limit? Why, the owners of hotels in the area, disgruntled that their sterile beer parlours were losing trade to John's wonderful new attraction.

Totally frustrated, John tried embarrassing the board. He asked why a popular success story like Spinnakers was held to the letter of the law when hotels engaged in all kinds of questionable activities, like receiving cash kickbacks from the Big Three brewers. The LCLB responded that it knew nothing of kickbacks; they were illegal and therefore did not exist. However, it was common for the big boys to give a $6 per keg kickback every month to favoured owners who sold a certain quantity of their beer. So John produced a cheque for $500 from Carling O'Keefe—Spinnakers' own kickback cheque—and called in a reporter. A photo of the cheque appeared in the paper along with a denial from the Carling O'Keefe sales manager that kickbacks existed, even though his signature was on the cheque. The government issued an edict and the kickbacks stopped. If you think John was applauded for forcing the Big Three and the government into the open with this, think again. What he got was the undying hatred of the BC Hotel Association, some of whose members had lost hundreds of dollars per month in kickbacks.

But John kept on battling, and eventually the LCLB granted him an expanded licence. Now Spinnakers was not only a popular success but making good money and financially sound. Then John was hit with an unpleasant development he couldn't digest: his two partners, seeing all the happy people in the pub and the money rolling in, wanted to franchise the Spinnakers name and operation in the United States. Apparently they weren't paying attention to what was happening with Colin Noble's attempts to franchise Nobleman Brewing Ltd. John wanted no part of this; he had his one perfect brewpub, so what else did he need? But when the other partners persisted and John held firm, they voted to buy him out and did so. This was a real tragedy for John, who had put so much of himself into Spinnakers.

In the end John had the grim satisfaction of seeing the utter failure of the Spinnakers franchise initiative. His ex-partners decided to create not one but two brewpubs in Seattle, a market that already had several established pub breweries and microbreweries. One of the new Spinnakers brewpubs was in an old church, the other in a shopping centre—neither of them prime locations for a pub. The brewing plants were poorly designed by the brewer John had trained at Spinnakers, who with just a year's experience as his sole brewing qualification was calling himself an "executive brewmaster." Too much hubris again! Without John to chase the details and veto bad decisions, shortcuts were taken that made the plants difficult to operate and the resultant beers unacceptable. Both Seattle operations closed about a year after opening, with huge losses. This blunder almost put the Spinnakers Victoria operation into receivership, but Paul Hadfield—the last of the three partners—managed to right the ship with the help of his brother. Today Spinnakers in Victoria is a much-expanded favourite watering hole, with the franchise disaster a very bad memory.

In Winnipeg things weren't going well for Colin Noble and his Friday's Bar experiment. Disappointed that the operation had not been an instant success and wasn't warmly embraced by the Winnipeg crowd, he closed it down and sold off the brewing plant. Lessons from the above—don't run before you can walk? Don't count your customers before you've tickled their palates? Do some market research before pitching your tent? According to Steve Jobs, Mike Markkula, who provided the $250,000 that brought the Apple II computer into being, advised that "you should never start a company with the goal of getting rich. Your goal should be making something you believe in and making a company that will last" (in *Steve Jobs*, by Walter Isaacson). He made a good point.

9 Brewing Plant Design

BY THE END OF THE 1980S I HAD BEEN CALLED IN TO oversee the start-up of eight brewpub or microbrewery plants, some with used equipment, some with new. Often my job was correcting issues in the plant design, construction, or layout that could have been avoided if these things had been thought out and corrected at the drawing-board stage. Eventually I decided to start designing my own plants and take no consulting job unless I had been involved from the very beginning with the owners, architects, builders, plumbers and electricians. Catching a problem before it's built into a brewery is far less costly in dollars and time than trying to correct it later.

One of the problem breweries I was asked to rescue was owned by Island Pacific Brewing on the outskirts of Victoria. It was a microbrewery that had been started up six months earlier but had yet to produce any saleable beer. It had been put together by a self-styled brewmaster whose background in brewing consisted of having worked as an hourly worker in Labatt's now-defunct Lucky Lager plant. He was seriously out of his depth as a brewery designer, and the owners had fired him when the defects started to emerge. When I was brought in, it was obvious to me that the wort heat-exchanger had been hooked up incorrectly. This was the kind of problem I could see and correct quite quickly, but I strongly suspected there were issues in this plant that I couldn't see, problems that were waiting to sneak up on me. For example, the plant had been built by a Victoria company that fitted out ships and did some stainless-steel fabrication on the side. It was ruggedly built, but unfortunately for us some of the welding was pretty rugged too. When I opened up the manway doors and looked inside the four 60-hectolitre (6,000-litre) cylindro-conical fermenters, I was dismayed at the rough quality of the welds. Someone had taken an angle grinder to them but only succeeded in adding scratches to the surface, and even the smallest scratch can hide a thousand beer-spoilage bacteria from the last brew. Nowadays "sanitary stainless-steel fabrication" is the name of the standard required in manufacturing hospital equipment and food plants, including breweries. It means that all welds are ground and polished to a 3A finish, that is, you should barely be able to *see* the welds, let alone detect any roughness when you run a finger over them. The welds inside these tanks were impossible to polish to 3A and therefore impossible to clean by the usual method of rinsing and then spraying sanitizer on the fermenter walls. Instead, I devised a system of filling the tanks with very hot water to sterilize them before introducing the new brew, but this cost time and money.

For a while I also lost sleep over the curious off flavour to the beer that I couldn't account for. The cold water coming from the tap was fine, but I could detect it in the hot water we used to make the brew. The hot water was stored in a large tank (a hot liquor tank) that received the water that had been used to cool the day's brew: this pre-heated water was stored and kept hot to be used to make the next day's brew. The tank worried me because it had no manway door, so there was no way to inspect the inside. I suppose the thinking had been that there was no need for one because it was just water in and water out. But when the odd flavour persisted, I hired a stainless welder and told him to cut a hole in the side of the hot liquor tank and install a manway door. When I stuck my head inside the hole, there was no doubt where that odd flavour was coming from: there was an inch of smelly black sludge on the bottom of the tank. Despite the fresh cold water being filtered, some fine sediment was obviously getting through, and the sludge had been building up and festering on the bottom of the tank since the brewery was started up—a nice legacy from the previous "brewmaster." After the tank was cleaned and the cold water filtration tightened up, the brew improved immediately. But that defect had cost us a lot of beer down the drain before I finally tracked it down.

I became very picky about welds and how they were finished. Many people judge a tank by how it looks on the outside. I learned to be more concerned about the inside. The thing is, TIG and MIG welding (that is, argon shield inert gas welding) is a thing of beauty in the hands of a professional and, when properly done, should require little in the way of grinding or polishing. Because the inert gas shields the arc from the atmosphere, there is no sparking, flashing or crackling—the only sound is the soft whistle of the argon shielding the tip of the electrode, which emits a tiny blue arc. The electrode holder is about the size of a marking pen and is held like a pen during the weld. If the parts to be joined have been ground so there is less than a millimetre gap between them, the welder does not even have to use the stainless "stick" to fill the gap; the arc will melt the metal on both sides of the join to make a nice, clean weld that is easy to polish. Use of a lot of stick usually means a lot of grinding and polishing. But getting welds to be acceptable for sanitary stainless work requires precision, a very steady hand and a lot of experience. Many welders say they can weld stainless, but fewer than one in ten can produce work of the standard required in brewing plant fabrication.

As I got more requests to act as consultant/designer on brewpubs and microbreweries, my approach changed a little. I began by talking to the prospective owners about what types of products they wanted—ales, lagers or both? And how many of each? What was the building like that the plant was going into? Did they have a floor plan? What services were available, such as the water supply and possible energy sources for firing the brew kettle? Were they prepared to dig up the floors to install drains and possibly a serving-line tunnel from finished beer tank area to pub bar? Had they considered a grain loft above the brewhouse for storing sacks of malt and housing the malt mill? (This is highly desirable as it gets the stored malt out of the way, keeps messy malt dust out of the brewhouse, and allows gravity feed from the mill to the mash tun below.) Is the brewery to be a showpiece or hidden away? What was the budget? My list of questions was long, and getting the answers before the project broke ground saved a lot of time and hassle later. Also, I was not selling them a brewing plant. I was selling them the services of a brewing professional who was going to design the floor plan and brewery, oversee construction, formulate the recipes, order ingredients, and see the project right through the first brews to a satisfactory finished product, including the interviewing and training of the brewer.

Back in the 1950s at Ardwick Tech I had taken technical drawing classes and passed the O level in that subject, but when I went into biology and microbiology I thought it was time wasted. I hadn't used those skills in over twenty years, but it's amazing how things lying dormant in your mind can be reawakened when you need them. Now I got myself a drawing board and soon my drawings of brewing vessels and other equipment and my lists of specifications covering every detail of the plant were getting favourable comments from the fabricators and engineers who had to interpret them. It made their jobs easier and left no room for doubt, no room for "Oh, you didn't tell me it had to be *that* way." And when I had produced my sheaf of drawings and specifications for every item in the plant, I sent them to three different stainless fabricators for quotes, not just one. And that is how I came to meet Ed Ripley of Ripley Stainless in Summerland, BC.

Ripley is the kind of fabricator you want to work with. He made tanks for the wineries in the Okanagan Valley, so he knew the standards implied by "sanitary stainless welding." In fact, it was the only type of welding he did, and he was a master at it. He welcomed my detailed drawings since they answered most of his questions, and if a problem came up, I was just a phone call away. Sometimes fabricators will want to make changes during the building of a plant, and since they are most often working to a contract price, these changes are often shortcuts to make the job easier (or cheaper) for them—not necessarily better. When I got a call from Ripley, it was usually because he had an idea that would improve the brewery plant. When it came to the installation, if the job site was within a day's drive of Summerland, he would always be there to do any on-site welding and see that the customer was satisfied. He was a super guy to work with. Over the next twenty years Ripley built ten brewing plants to my designs, all of them still operating.

As an example of how he would make things better, Ripley introduced me to German DIN fittings. The screw-thread fittings that connect transfer hoses to tanks are prime suspects for introducing bacterial contamination and are specially made to sanitary standards. In those days most of the established breweries in North America were using American Dairy Thread, the female side having a large hex nut that required a wrench and the rubber gasket that sealed the connection being a loose item. This posed a problem, as you almost needed three hands to make the connection without the gasket dropping on the floor and picking up contaminants—or rolling down the drain. The DIN fitting deals with this problem by having the gasket fit snugly into the male side of the coupling so it never drops out. In addition, these couplings are so well engineered that you can get a good seal just by tightening the round nut by hand, a wrench rarely being needed. Ripley started importing these fittings because he saw that they were the best, and he knew that's what I wanted on my plants. After that, all of them had DIN fittings.

Some manufacturers of small brewing plants seem to have a cookie-cutter approach to design: one plant fits all. The trouble with that approach is there are so many different shapes and sizes of buildings a brewery has to be fitted into, different energy sources available, different owners wanting different products. The list is such that the only valid approach is to carefully study the site and services; talk to the owners, architects, builders and journeymen; and then design the plant accordingly. In one brewpub I had a small freight elevator installed to lift the pallets of bagged malt to the upper floor grain loft. Occasionally I come across an owner who says, "Couldn't the brewer just *carry* the sacks upstairs?" I usually ask them if they would like to try packing a 25-kilogram (or even 50-kilogram) sack of malt up two flights of stairs and then repeat that twenty or thirty times. A day's brewing is hard enough as it is, and I am always thinking of how to design the brewery to make the brewer's life easier. If owners insist on saving money by having their brewers do unnecessary grunt work, I walk away from the project. On another job, a spiral staircase was my answer to getting the brewer up and down in a three-level layout. The layout in yet another situation was so awkward for getting the malt to where it was required that I did away with bagged malt and put in a grain bulk tank with a pneumatic delivery system. This cost almost $20,000 but saved the brewer from quitting, stressed out from overwork. (It *has* happened.)

Energy sources or a lack of them can require creative solutions. Natural gas is the cheapest and the best for brewery purposes, but sometimes it's not available. This was the case with Swans, established in 1989 in old-town Victoria, and Yaletown in Vancouver. The answer was three-phase electrical power with massive immersion heaters in the brew kettle. This would scare many brewers anxious that direct contact between the heating elements and the wort would result in scorching, but the answer to this problem is the use of elements with a low watt density similar to those used to heat fruit juices. They are much larger and more expensive than those used to heat water but are able to boil the wort without changing its flavour.

A natural gas burner can be used to heat the kettle directly, as we did in the Horseshoe Bay Brewery, but this is not recommended except for the simplest, smallest plants because a lot of heat is wasted and dissipated into the brewhouse, making it uncomfortably hot. The heat from the burner can also be blown through a flame tube, a four-inch-diameter loop of stainless pipe inside the kettle. While this works fairly well, by far the best use of natural gas is to generate steam in a separate small boiler. In this set-up the steam heats the kettle by passing through stainless jackets attached to the outside of its floor and walls, giving very even, controlled heating. And having steam available also means you can heat the mash tun via steam jackets, so the mash is treated to a series of "upward step" thermal plateaus at, say, 50°C, 65°C and 75°C (122°F, 149°F and 167°F). This produces more fermentable extract and better lagers than those made from a single-temperature (65°C) infusion mash, which is more suitable for ales. Steam is also useful for sterilizing other equipment, particularly kegs and filling machines.

At Swans other problems arose because the only location for the brewery was slap bang in the middle of an old building that was being transformed into a hotel, a restaurant, kitchens, a cold beer and wine store, and a pub. The three-phase electrical cable to power the brew kettle was over a hundred feet long and cost $5,000. As well, there was the little problem of how to get the vent stack from the kettle to the outside world. Above the brewery were two floors of hotel guest rooms and around it on every side were all manner of other activities, so there was no way to vent the vapour when the kettle was boiling. After thinking it through, I came up with a design for a condenser—an eight-inch-diameter section of pipe, blanked at the far end, that fitted onto the vent stack with one-inch stainless tubes running in parallel inside it, carrying cold water to condense the steam as it passed. It worked very well (and still does) and we were able to do without an outside vent. As custom stainless work does not come cheap, Michael Williams, the owner of Swans, was none too happy with the unforeseen costs of the electrical cable and the condenser, but there was no help for it. The building was dictating the brewery design.

I always ask prospective brewery owners if they have a preference for whole hops or pellets, since it affects the design of the plant. As hop oils deteriorate steadily from the time the hop is picked, whole hops must be kept under refrigeration, and since they usually come in 200-pound bales, no ordinary refrigerator will do the trick; a large insulated room must be built to hold them, cooled to just above freezing. Hop pellets, which are vacuum-sealed in aluminum/plastic sachets, deteriorate far more slowly than whole hops and require less storage space: two 40-pound boxes of pellets will contain more hop oils and resins than a 200-pound bale of whole hops. For these reasons, many brewers have moved to the use of pellets in the last thirty years.

However, the decision to go with pellets over whole hops also makes a difference to the brewer's workload, as the spent hops have to be removed from the brew after the wort has been boiled with the hops to extract the bittering and flavouring oils. This is a messy business if you use whole hops, but much simplified with hop pellets. Whole hops are removed in a hop back, a flat vessel with a screen in the bottom to strain out the hops, which are removed manually after the brew is pumped out. Hop pellets are reduced to powder in the boil and form a sludge with the trub (the proteins and tannins precipitated out of solution by boiling). This sludge is removed in a whirlpool tank, which was invented by engineers at Molson. In this set-up the wort from the kettle is pumped at high velocity into the tank through a nozzle that parallels the vessel wall. This results in the entire brew rotating inside the tank, then as the brew slows and settles, the sludge is deposited in a shallow cone in the centre of the tank floor. After the brew has been pumped out, the sludge is easily cleaned out with a hose and flushed down the drain.

Having tasted and analyzed a lot of beer samples in my O'Keefe days during that company's switch from whole hops to pellets, I have to say that the prejudice of traditionalists against pellets on the grounds of beer quality and flavour are not justified. If educated taste buds and chromatography cannot discern any differences, that's good enough for me. Having said this, if your brewery is close to a hop-growing area so that you can get fresh hops in season that still have the wonderful aromatics that are lost in storage, by all means use them. Just don't boil the hell out of them, or you will lose all those light, volatile molecules up the vent stack. Add them in the hop back or whirlpool *after the boil,* or "dry hop" the beer in cold storage or in the cask.

Fermenters come in many different shapes and sizes that are suited to different products and building limitations. They can be as simple as a single-wall upright cylinder with an open top, which is suitable for ales, like the one John Mitchell and I started with at Horseshoe Bay. As we had no built-in refrigeration, if the brew was getting too warm in the summer, we threw a copper coil into the fermenter and circulated cold water through it. The best fermenting cellar employing open fermenters I have seen was one in northern California that utilized a separate sterile room with positive air pressure and UV light to keep the air sterile. Nobody was allowed inside except the brewer, and he had to wash his boots and gloves in sanitizer before entering. On the other hand, the fermenter can be as complex (and expensive) as a modern cylindro-conical or unitank type rated for 20 psi pressure that is totally enclosed, has digital temperature control, a built-in cleaning system and multiple jackets on the outside walls carrying refrigerant. In this single set-up you can ferment the brew, cool it, draw off the deposited yeast, carbonate the beer and age it, saving the cost of separate tanks for aging and mitigating the initial high cost of the unitank. More importantly, it is a sealed system that obviates the risk of aerial contamination. An infected brew that you have to sewer costs a lot in terms of ingredients, labour and aging time, and as the brew size increases, the cost looms larger. This is why I have given up on open fermenters—even ones with lids—if they are to be located in the brewhouse or other open areas that are swirling with micro-organisms. The extra cost of closed fermenters is paid for by not having to buy separate aging tanks, avoids spoiled beer, and reduces expenditures on bought CO_2, since you can naturally carbonate the beer in the fermenter as you cool it in the latter stages of fermentation. With these modern fermenters you have lost the option of using the old-fashioned top-fermenting ale yeasts, which we used in Horseshoe Bay, but there are now "bottom-settling" ale yeasts (if that's not a contradiction in terms) that give very satisfactory results.

Storage beer tanks (also known as serving or bright tanks) are single-wall upright cylinders kept in a refrigerated room. They are not usually given a high polish on the outside of the tank like those in more visible brewing plants, since they are most often hidden away in the cold room. But once again, polished welds are more important on the inside of the tank than the outside. You need at least two storage tanks for each product you brew, one aging while the other is prepared for serving/kegging/bottling. I am in favour of as little filtration as possible, preferably none, which gives a much fuller flavour and more body to the beer. In brewpub situations it is quite possible to get acceptably clear beer by dosing it with isinglass finings as it is transferred from fermenter to storage to serving tank. Isinglass is a colloid that will slowly settle to the bottom of the tank, taking yeast cells and protein particles with it. I use short (four-to-six-inch) upstand pipes or risers that fit into the bottom outlet of the tank, so that the clear beer is decanted off from above the sediment on the tank bottom. Serving the beer directly from the tank to the bar eliminates the work of kegging and dealing with kegs.

Storage beer tanks are usually fitted with a carbonating "stone," similar to a large fish tank aeration device, which releases a fine cloud of CO_2 into the beer to bring up the carbonation level if it is too low. As cellars containing single-wall tanks are temperature-controlled and therefore kept closed, there is a problem with the buildup of the CO_2 released from fermentations and from tanks when they are emptied. This CO_2 increase in the air can cause dizziness, and in extreme cases unconsciousness and death. Therefore, a small amount of air exchange is essential to suck the CO_2 out and replenish it with fresh air, and since CO_2 is heavier than air, the exhaust from the cellar has to be located *at the lowest point* of the cellar wall.

When I was growing up in England, draft Guinness was widely available in pubs, but my dad would say, "Yes, but the best pint of Guinness is within ten miles of St. James's Gate." This is where the Guinness brewery was located in Dublin, and it was the only place where cask-conditioned Guinness was available. Cask conditioning means producing the CO_2 in the finished beer by inducing a secondary fermentation in the cask. When you do this, the CO_2 dissolves in the beer and is held more tightly than if you carbonate the beer with CO_2 from an outside source. When you serve the beer—or in this case, stout—the bubbles are much smaller and more voluminous than those of "brewery conditioned" beers, contributing to a better, longer-lasting head. Of course, that is not the only reason for that creamy head the barman can sculpt a shamrock in. Guinness is brewed with large amounts of roasted malts and roasted barley, which give it that black colour, but they also have another effect: roasting the grains burns the starchy part so that it now contributes little to the fermentable extract but instead yields a mixture of complex compounds called melanoidins, which are not fermented but add to the body or specific gravity of the finished beer. This increases the surface tension, and the result is a much improved head that will last a long time.

The problem with cask-conditioned beers is that they do not travel well, as they contain the yeast sediment from that final fermentation. To serve clear beer and leave the sediment behind, the cask must be "fined" with isinglass finings and then "stillaged" on its side for three or more days before tapping. This was all part of the bar cellarman's art in bygone days, but today few pubs or bar staff have time for this finicky business. They want casks or kegs that contain finished, clear, carbonated beer that is ready to serve as soon as delivered and tapped. The brewery responds with brewery-conditioned beer that is filtered for clarity, and the final carbonation is added from a tank of liquid CO_2. But stout produced like this does not have the same creamy head. This is an issue that Guinness wrestled with for many years. You could buy Guinness around the world, but those in the know would moan, "Ah, but it's not the same as St. James's Gate Guinness!" The company's answer was rather high-tech: instead of serving the stout by pushing it through conventional beer taps with pure CO_2, they used a mixture of CO_2 and nitrogen gas and invented a unique Guinness tap that restricted the flow to promote foaming. Nitrogen gas is hard to dissolve in liquids, but once in, it is slow to come out. The result was that trademark creamy head that leaves a lacework of foam down the glass as you drink. You have to hand it to Guinness: they weren't going to settle for an inferior product and unhappy drinkers even if it required inventing a new (and exclusive) way of serving their stout. They have gone to even greater lengths to reproduce the same effect in their canned stout by introducing a widget into the can. The widget is a small plastic sphere that contains liquid nitrogen mixed with a small amount of beer, which is released through a tiny hole as soon as the can is opened. Just don't try it unless you have a glass handy and the can is thoroughly chilled.

Many brewery owners want a copper kettle, having seen beautiful examples in Europe or older breweries elsewhere, but they rapidly change their minds when they realize that it would be worth a king's ransom with the price of copper these days. Copper was the material of choice for kettles for centuries—in fact, in British breweries the brew kettle was simply called "the copper," and it is still called that, even when most are now made of stainless steel. Copper was chosen first because its relative softness gave it the ductility to be rolled and drawn into the shapes required. Second, the heat transference of copper is more than twice that of stainless steel, giving a faster, better boil. And third, it does not rust like mild steel. It does oxidize, producing a greenish-black verdigris, but since the pH of wort is slightly acidic, when the wort is boiled, a tiny amount of the surface layer of the copper is dissolved and the inside of the kettle is "shined" with every brew. But keeping the visible outside upper dome clean is nearly a full-time job for the brewer. There was quite a debate among brewmasters when stainless kettles began to replace copper vessels, since it was known that small amounts of copper ions in the wort had the effect of suppressing bacterial growth and thus helped in preventing spoilage. But in the age of stainless steel, excellent cleaning methods and tight quality control have eliminated the need for the bacteriostatic effect of copper. Still, one older brewmaster I knew, whose whole career had been with copper kettles and who now found himself in charge of a shiny new stainless plant, had a thin strip of copper foil inserted discreetly between the plates of the wort heat-exchanger, hedging his bets on the worth of a trace of copper in the brew.

However, it is the beauty of copper that is paramount to some owners, and this has led to the use of copper-faced cladding on brewhouse vessels. This cladding is what holds the heat insulation around the inner vessel, and it's made from 16-gauge stainless steel with a thin coating of copper. To satisfy an owner who must have that coppery look to his brewhouse, I have on occasion specified "copper-clad" vessels while inwardly regretting all the extra work I'm making for the brewer in trying to keep his brewery polished up. Just a splash of caustic soda that is not immediately washed off will result in a black stain on that beautiful copper, and scrubbing this off will often remove the copper too, since it is less than a millimetre thick. My advice to brewery owners: stick to stainless.

Though often overlooked, getting the right mill and the right grind is very important to a brewer. You want to grind the starchy part of the grain to a coarse flour while keeping the husk in pieces that are as large as possible. This sounds like a contradiction, and it is, but trying to achieve the perfect grind is the reason big breweries pay hundreds of thousands of dollars for a mill specifically designed for the purpose. These are large four- or six-roller mills, with the first two rollers set to just crack the seed so that the husk falls off. Beaters and a current of air then blow the husk out of the grist stream, to be reintroduced after the second and third rollers grind the remainder to the desired particle size. The reason you want the pieces of husk unground is that it is the insoluble husk that holds the grain bed apart when the liquid sweet wort is extracted from the mash during the runoff. No husk, and you have a mash of sticky porridge that will gum up the separation of liquid from solid. Small breweries don't have the money or space for a six-roller mill and mostly use two-roller types, but there are many models available and it's worth spending a bit more to get one with an easily adjustable roller gap that you can reset even while the mill is running. If the recipe calls for the use of specialty or "colouring" malts, you will need to grind these finer than the main body of pale malt. One roller should be driven by the motor, the other free, and the driven one should be machined with grooves to catch the seeds. Checking the grind should be done every brew when "mashing in." To take a sample, hold your hand out flat with the fingers together and let the grist stream over them. Moving your fingers slightly will separate the particles. No unground grains should be there. Nice big pieces of husk? The starchy endosperm mostly ground to particles one to two millimetres in size with not too much fine flour? Excellent!

10 Brewing in the USA

The Humboldt Brewery

In 1986 I was installing a microbrewery in Edmonton when I got a call from a man in Arcata, in northern California. He told me his name was Mario Celotto, that he had been a linebacker in the NFL with the Buffalo Bills and the Oakland Raiders and had been coaching a college team in Arcata. But he had plans to open a pub—or, rather, a brewpub. He had been looking through some brewing magazines and saw my name mentioned, and he was wondering if he could hire me as consultant brewmaster on the project. Could he fly up and talk to me about it? I was somewhat surprised that he had tracked me down in Edmonton, since I was based in the Kootenays, and explained that I was going to be there for a month or two, but he wasn't put off and said he would arrive in Edmonton in a few days. And so he did.

Mario was a genial giant of a man, full of smiles and a big fan of "real beer," as he put it. He had photos of the building he had acquired for the pub in downtown Arcata, and we went over the plans and discussed options. By the time he left a day later, I had agreed to sign on to the project and get to work on designing the plant as soon as I got home. The work went on throughout that winter, with me designing the plant to a floor plan that Mario sent me. When the drawings were complete, I sent them to various fabricators for quotes. Ripley Stainless had the advantage of a low Canadian dollar over US fabricators, but I also asked for a quote from SPR in England, as they had built the brewing plants for Spinnakers in Victoria and Friday's Bar in Winnipeg. Their quote was only $3,200 higher than Ripley's, but then there was about $10,000 to be added for shipping the plant from England to California, plus the difficulty of getting spare parts sent out quickly from the UK, something that had been a problem in Winnipeg. So Ripley got the job. We saved money by buying a dozen 800-litre used storage tanks from a dealer in England and then sized the brewing plant accordingly. I was glad Ed Ripley had gotten the nod, as his location in Summerland was just a half-day's drive from my home, allowing me to check on progress as the plant was built.

When the plant was completed in March 1987, the large vessels were sent to Arcata by commercial transport, while I was to take the three dozen loose items—pumps, valves, custom pipework, sight glasses, oxygenator and carbonator, hoses and fittings, diverter panel, pump dolly, heat-exchanger, hydrometer cylinder, seals and wrenches—south to California in my pickup. This load of stainless fittings was worth $11,200, and as I didn't want any hangups at the border, I had asked Ripley to have all the correct customs declarations prepared. With the documentation and everything packed in my truck, I left Summerland and headed south. I was ready for the USA—or so I thought.

TOP Horseshoe Bay Brewery, 1982. We got our federal license from government officials. John Mitchell puffs out his cheeks in a sigh of relief, Frank Appleton raises a fist—another hurdle cleared! *Photo Jenny Mitchell*

BOTTOM Horseshoe Bay Brewery, 1982. Frank Appleton and John Mitchell at the brewing plant—opened in midsummer and it was hot! Even hotter in the brewhouse. *Photo Jenny Mitchell*

TOP LEFT	Horseshoe Bay Brewery, 1982. John Mitchell kegging up.
	Photo Frank Appleton
TOP RIGHT	Horseshoe Bay Brewery, 1982. Frank Appleton pitches 1313 yeast
	into first brew. A traditional English top-fermenting yeast, long
	asleep in the archives of the National Collection of Yeast Cultures.
	Photo John Mitchell
BOTTOM	Horseshoe Bay Brewery, 1982. John Mitchell and Frank Appleton
	cleaning kegs in Mitchell's backyard—the less appealing of brewery
	jobs. Note John's rock work. *Photo Jenny Mitchell*

Dave Patrick, John Mitchell, Frank Appleton, Don Rose celebrate the birth of Bay Ale, June 1982. Dave and Don were John's partners at the Troller Pub. Vancouver Sun *photo by Ralph Bowen*

TOP LEFT   Swans Brewpub, 1989. Sean Hoyne in brewery. Sean was a great student of brewing who went on to own his own brewery, making really fine beers. *Photo Frank Appleton*

TOP RIGHT   Spinnakers, 1984. Appleton cleaning out Brew Kettle. A sweaty, smelly business, but it's part of the job. *Photo John Mitchell*

BOTTOM   Humboldt Brewery, 1987. Left to right: John Demarinis, Mario Celotto, Frank Appleton, and helper. *Photo Jean Bassett*

TOP Swans Brewpub, 1989. Left to right: Michael Williams, Frank Appleton and unknown BC liquor board official, who had just delivered our licence, celebrate opening. *Photo courtesy of the author*

BOTTOM Swans Brewpub, 1989. Frank Appleton pulls the first pints for Michael Williams and liquor board official after receiving licence. *Photo courtesy of the author*

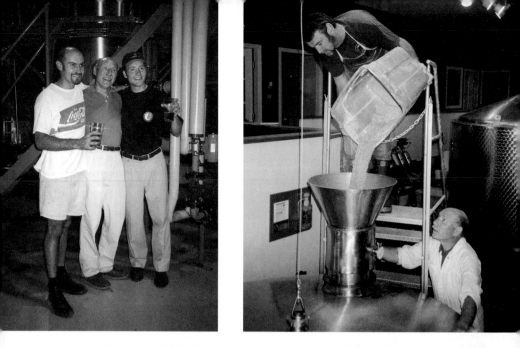

TOP LEFT   Ninkasi Ale House, Lyon, 1997. Christophe Fargier, Frank Appleton and Kurt Huffmann. *Photo Jean Bassett*

TOP RIGHT   Tin Whistle Brewing Company, 1995. "Mashing in": Richard Grierson pours in grist while Frank Appleton monitors hydrator, which is spraying hot water on the grist stream to create the mash. *Photo Laurie Lock*

BOTTOM   The Brewhouse, Whistler, BC., 2002. Frank Appleton in the Brewhouse brewing facility. *Photo Lin Clifton*

Yaletown Brewing Co., 2002. Frank Appleton back in the storage cellar again as a tourist! *Photo Lin Clifton*

TOP   Swans Brewing Appleton Brown Ale. Michael Williams insisted that one of the first line of "permanent" beers that went on tap at Swans be named after Frank. He chose the Brown Ale as a tip of the hat to his north England background.

BOTTOM   Hoyne Brewing Appleton ESB Label. Sean Hoyne surprised Frank in 2015 by asking if he could name a beer after him, and Appleton ESB was launched in October—a great honour from Frank's former trainee, now an accomplished brewmaster with his own brewery.

I rolled up to the US customs post at Oroville, Washington, and proudly presented my sheaf of paperwork. The officer looked through it, came out and checked what was in my truck, ticked off the items, and then we went back into the office, where the amount of duty was calculated. The payment would be made through a customs agent Mario had hired in Oroville. All the items were cleared, but then the officer said that his superior, the chief customs officer, wanted a word with me. I went into his office and he asked me to take a seat as he leafed through the documents.

"Everything seems to be in order, Frank," he said, "but may I ask what *your* role is in this project?"

"Well," I said, "I'm the designer and the brewing consultant, and I'm going down to Arcata to hook the plant up and get it brewing."

"You being paid for this?" he asked.

"Well, of course!" I replied naively.

"You have a green card to enable you to work in the States?" he persisted.

"No," I said apprehensively.

"Well, in that case you are not allowed to work in this country, and I have to refuse you entry."

I was stunned. I had taken so much care with the paperwork for the fittings but hadn't given a thought to myself. My tail between my legs, I got in my truck and retreated to Oliver on the Canadian side and got a hotel room. My mind was in a whirl. Those guys in Arcata would never be able to put the plant together without me—none of them had even worked in a brewery. I put in a call to Mario, and he was similarly stunned. "Wait there till I call you back," he said. An hour or two passed before he called. He had spoken to his customs agent, and they had arranged to send a former US customs officer across the border to talk to me. When he arrived, he surprised me with his plan to get me out of this dilemma.

"What we need is to find you a customs post that hasn't heard of you," he said, "and you go there, present your papers, say you are just a driver taking this shipment down and coming back." This from a retired customs officer! "You're lucky," he added, "that it's Friday. The customs posts on the US side close to Vancouver will be swamped with Canadians going south to buy cheap booze and gas. The customs will be so busy they won't have time to fuss with you. So you drive down to one of the border posts in the Fraser Valley, join the lineup of Canucks looking for a good time, go into the trucking lane, present your papers, and remember—you're just the driver. You don't say *anything* about working!"

It worked like a charm. There was quite a lineup at the Aldergrove crossing, but I parked my truck and took my customs declarations into the office. The harried officer flipped through the pages, made a note of our customs agent and the amount due, had me sign a paper saying I was the driver responsible for delivery of the shipment, stamped the pages, and I was on my way. As I drove south, I made a mental note to follow the rest of the instructions given to me by that retired US customs officer and set up my own company as soon as I got home. It would bill my clients and then pay me in Canada, so that I could say yes, I was installing equipment down there, but it was Canadian equipment and I was working and being paid in Canadian dollars by a Canadian company. Whew!

Two days later, after driving through the incredible redwood forests of northern California, I arrived in Arcata. Mario, his friends and helpers were delighted to see me safe and sound, not stuck in some border jail for attempting illegal entry. The area for the brewery had been prepared with the drains, water and gas supplies installed exactly as I had laid out in my drawings. What a difference from the unpleasant surprises of the Winnipeg operation three years earlier! We set to work assembling the Humboldt Brewery. The whole crew was infectiously enthusiastic, and when I remarked on this, they said, "Hey, why wouldn't we be? We're building a *brewery*!" And the work went very smoothly.

One of the differences in the States was the attitude of the licensing authorities compared to the parsimonious provincial liquor boards in Canada, who treat licences to make and sell beer as if they were licences to make explosives and applicants as possible miscreants. I went with Mario when he applied for his licence, and the official could hardly have been more helpful: "What is it you want to do? Build a brewpub? What is that? Brew your own beer for your pub? Oh, what a great idea! Just what Arcata needs. Well, fill out these forms here, and when we've checked you out and you've paid the fee, you'll have your licence. Just remember to pay your excise taxes or some guys with guns will be after you, and don't come crying to us if you go broke. But hey—best of luck!" There were no restrictions on the number of seats the pub could have—if the fire marshal approved, then it was okay. The difference between the attitudes of the authorities in Canada and those in the States could drive you to drink.

Mario had hired John Demarinis, who had done some college science, as the trainee brewer. John was your typical laid-back, easygoing Californian and was delighted to have the job. He and I got along very well. Enthusiasm is certainly a great start for a brewer in any operation, and showing your enthusiasm for beer to your public is a must for a craft brewer. When taking a picture of John at the test bench with its hydrometers, thermometers and glassware, a reporter asked John how he measured the quality of his beers. "By the width of your smile" was his reply.

I liked Arcata. A small college town (Humboldt State), it was full of young people who were interested in what we were doing and eager to try the product. Mario only wanted to produce ales, which simplified things for me, and have them served at the correct temperature (45°F) via traditional English hand pumps, which we imported along with British specialty malts and the 8 hectolitre (HL) beer tanks. Here's the description of the beers from the menu of the Humboldt Brewery, launched in the first week of June 1987:

> Welcome to Humboldt County's first-ever
> Brewpub. We are delighted to offer you the
> following selection of authentic English ales. All
> our ales are made from 100% malt mash with
> no adjuncts or additives and are not filtered
> or pasteurized. Beer like this is high in soluble
> protein and vitamins—it is a meal in itself. Our
> recipes are combinations of American Klages
> 2-row malt with British crystal, chocolate and
> wheat malts, laced with the resins of Eroica,
> Cascade and Willamette Kent Golding hops. The

ales range in color from golden to darkest brown and in palate from moderately light to very full-bodied. The alcohol content ranges from 4.5% to 5.4% by volume. Special brews may exceed this.

The menu went on to describe the three flagship brews: Gold Rush Pale Ale, Red Nectar Ale ("a robust, red, fruity flower of a beer") and Storm Cellar Porter ("a rich, nutty, coffee-colored porter whose heavy gravity and potent alcohol make it the perfect drink for taking refuge when you have no place to go").

I couldn't have said it better. This is how you want to talk about your beers—with pride and a bit of humour too—and to do that, you have to produce beers that you're proud of. I was pleased with the performance of the plant, and Mario and his pals rejoiced. The opening bash he threw to launch the pub was packed, with some of his old NFL linemen buddies towering over the rest of us. Even John and Jenny Mitchell showed up for the opening, plus a carload with my partner, Jean Bassett, and other folks all the way from the Kootenays. We had a great time. The only thing I didn't care for on the menu was Mario's specialty: Buffalo chicken wings, which were doused in a red-hot pepper sauce he had discovered while playing for the Buffalo Bills. They were so hot they brought tears to my eyes, and no amount of beer would cool my seared gullet. Mario was a bit dismayed at my reaction, but I explained that I came from England, a land noted for its dull, non-spicy food.

I liked the layout of the Humboldt pub. It had three rooms—the bar and two rooms with booths, snug places where you could enjoy a meal with friends away from the noise. The barroom boasted a 25-foot-long, antique, solid oak bar, a piece of the Old West that Mario had found somewhere. Sitting at the bar, you could catch a glimpse of the brewery through the windows behind it, but the brewer wasn't in a goldfish-bowl situation because Mario had the plate glass decorated with etched motifs of hops and barley. A nice operation all around, and with great beers too, by the time I headed back to Canada.

Postscript: The Humboldt Brewery operated in Arcata from 1987 to 2003, when the brewing plant and its brand-name products were sold to the Firestone Walker brewery in Paso Robles, California, where Humboldt's line of "nectar beers" are still produced. In 2004 a group of former Humboldt employees leased the building in Arcata and reopened as a pub/restaurant featuring live music. The brewhouse area is now a dance floor.

Deschutes: From a ten-barrel brewpub to a 300,000 barrel per year craft brewery

It didn't take long before I got another call from the States. It was 1988. The caller was Gary Fish, and he and his father were interested in starting a brewpub in Bend, Oregon. Was I available to act as their consultant? When I asked why they had chosen me, Gary said they had been looking at the new brewpubs that were springing up in California and liked what they saw at the Humboldt Brewery. Mario had suggested they call me.

Now, I had been through Bend on my way to California in the 1960s and wouldn't have thought it qualified on any count as "location, location, location." I remembered it as a sleepy little lumber mill and livestock town with a sparse population in the high semi-desert country in the middle of Oregon. There was literally nothing of note around Bend, save for some extinct volcanoes, Mount Bachelor being the highest. Since Gary told me he had grown up in California, I wondered why he wasn't thinking of locating there, as California was a hotbed of the burgeoning craft beer movement. "We were thinking of it," he said, "but property values have just gone crazy there, and there are already a number of craft breweries established." And he explained that in recent years Bend had been reinventing itself as a second home and playground for the well-to-do from the Portland and San Francisco Bay areas and now offered golf courses, tennis courts, canoeing on the Deschutes River, rock climbing, mountain biking and skiing in the winter— as well as inexpensive land for building. Gary and his father were smart business people, and they saw how the town's population was growing, mainly due to tourism. (When I had passed through there in the '60s, the population was about 12,000; by the time we opened the brewpub in 1988, it had almost doubled, and in 2013 it was estimated at over 81,000.) Gary had acquired a building on Bond Street, the main street of the town, and they were completely rebuilding it as a pub. Was I interested? "Send me a floor plan and an analysis of the Bend water supply," I replied, thinking of that semi-desert country. But the lab report on the water was quite good.

Figuring out the size of the plant was the first thing. There is no point in going to a brew size smaller than 10 HL (1,000 litres) if you want to make money at it, because if you are a success, you will be brewing around the clock just trying to keep up with the demand. If the brewery is designed for it, one person can look after a brew of 10, 20 or even 50 HL, and the unit cost of brewing a litre of beer decreases dramatically as the brew size goes up. But Gary's brewery area was limited to one large room behind the pub/restaurant section of his building with a cold room off to one side; above it would be a malt storage area with the malt mill. Taking all of this into account, we decided on a brew size of 10 BBL (barrel) US, which is approximately 12 HL or 1,200 litres. At the time I wondered how we were going to sell all this beer in the tiny town of Bend. But five years later the plant was being pushed beyond its limit, producing four or five brews a day, and Gary and his dad were calling on me to help design a brand-new 50 BBL brewery (more about that later).

How did this happen? Certainly, much of it had to do with Gary's careful planning and hard work and the great crew of people he attracted. Before undertaking this project, he had spent twelve years running a restaurant in Salt Lake City, so he already knew the importance of good food to a brewpub. Then he had attended the Brewing School at the University of California at Davis, not because he intended to brew himself but so he could understand the process. You've got to like an owner with an attitude like that. But his operation would have remained small if its sales had been limited to the Bend area. What made it really take off was sales of keg beer to other licensees and, eventually, bottled beer to the public. Once again I saw the differences between the overly protective liquor laws in Canada and the open, free-enterprise attitude in the US. In British Columbia, if you were granted a brewpub licence, you could only sell your beer in your pub, not to other licensees—a situation that inhibited the growth of brewpub beers until the law was finally changed in 2001. In the western states the attitude was "You want to sell your beer to other outlets? Go ahead!"

Gary chose to use whole hops, and this choice made sense given the proximity of Bend to the major hop growing areas in the Willamette Valley. So a hop back was included in my package of drawings, replacing the whirlpool tank that I would have prescribed in a location using hop pellets. I decided to install closed fermenters to guard against aerial contamination in the busy brewhouse area. The kettle was direct-fired with a natural gas burner. The mash tun was not heated, so all the brews were of a single-temperature infusion mash, although we did get a little extra heating from the final sparging, where hot water is sprayed onto the mash to rinse out the last of the extract. Once again, Ripley Stainless got the nod for the fabrication.

Gary had hired John Harris, a brewer with experience in small breweries, to take over the brewing so that he could focus on the kitchen and running the business. John and I got along well, and the start-up went smoothly in the summer of 1988. The grand opening featured a "yard of ale" drinking contest; the only person who could finish it was the huge construction boss we had on the job. After I left, the Deschutes brewpub started to win over the bland-beer drinkers of Bend. Here is how Gary put it in the 1999 Brewers' Market Guide:

> The brewpub itself won customers in Bud-drinking Bend because we were determined and our quality was good. Bars in Bend suffered from what I call "institutionalized mediocrity." Average was the standard toward which everyone aspired. We never accepted that, and time has proven us

right. We believed that customers should have as many reasons as possible to visit the pub. The food, the beer, the atmosphere, the service, the music, our community activities—we paid attention to everything. The beer was great, but that alone would not be enough. There was also an element of luck. I have said many times [that] everyone should at least once in their lives be in the right place at the right time, and we were.

But sometimes your luck runs out. In December of that first year a batch went bad in fermentation from an unknown infection. Gary had no choice but to dump it and brew again. This also went bad. Then another, and another, and another. They dumped ten straight brews down the drain while getting more and more frantic. They tried to get me to come down, but I was totally committed in Victoria, planning the brewery in the Swans Hotel. Gary and John then enlisted another consultant, and they tore the brewery apart to find the problem. It turned out to be infected malt dust hanging up in the grist leg that delivered the grist (ground malt) from the mill to the mash tun below. Because it had not been possible to locate the mill directly over the mash tun, we had angled a four-inch plastic pipe through the brewhouse wall to carry the grist, but the angle was not steep enough to completely empty it after "mashing-in." Steam from the mashing was rising up this pipe and moistening the residual grist, which then produced a rich growth of mould and other nasty organisms. When these spores hit that nice warm mash, they were growing like crazy and having a ball! Every batch was infected at its inception. As the grist leg had been built into the wall when the room was finished, it had not been possible to inspect, remove, or clean it as part of the regular maintenance, so the nasties had been accumulating for months. After the grist leg was replaced and the mouldy malt dust completely eradicated, the beer returned to normal, and Gary wrote afterward:

> The dumped batches did not create a public-relations problem for us because we hadn't released any substandard beer. In fact, we used the incident to illustrate our commitment to quality and show how we had put that philosophy to the test.

After this near disaster their wholesale business began to grow. People who came to vacation in Bend liked the beer, and when they went home to Portland, San Francisco or Seattle, they asked for Deschutes beers at their local taverns, and Gary began getting calls from pub owners and beverage distributors. People were coming to buy Deschutes beer without any sales pitch or marketing. As I have said to some of my trainee brewers: "Let the product speak for itself." One bold decision Gary made was to feature Black Butte Porter as their lead brand. He wrote:

> We believed in the product. We saw that, whereas the market for dark beers was smaller than that for light beers, everyone was competing for the lighter beer market. We believed we could dominate the porter market. Today Black Butte Porter is the second-largest-selling porter in the US and holds a 73% share of the porter market in Oregon.

In 1993 the little 10 BBL system in Bend, Oregon, pushed to 12.5 BBL, cranking out 7,200 BBL of beer in an average of 11 different brews per week. The place was bursting at the seams, despite leasing an adjacent building for warehouse space. They were loading semi-trailer trucks on downtown streets, and the city wasn't happy. Something had to be done. Gary and his dad were facing a new reality: they were making far more money from their keg sales than from the brewpub. They made a momentous—and risky—decision: they would build a 50 BBL brewery from scratch. My phone began ringing again.

In my thirty years of consulting and designing twenty brewing systems, the Deschutes Brewery project was the only one where the building was designed around the brewery, not the other way around. This was not a brewpub, as Gary retained the original outlet on Bond Street. This was to be a 50 BBL production brewery. Gary had decided we would build a vertical tower brewery, which is traditionally how they were built before electric pumps were invented. Gravity flow would move the wort and beer in process from one level to the next because the gentler the transfer, the better the beer will like it. The idea is to have the malt mill on the uppermost floor so that the ground malt (grist) drops through the floor to the mash tun below. When the mash is converted, the sweet wort is run by gravity to the brew kettle, and after the wort is boiled, it is run through a plate heat-exchanger to the fermenting floor below. After fermentation, the beer is transferred to storage and finishing tanks on the lowest level, where bottling and kegging also take place. The entire facility would be over 65,000 square feet on nearly four acres of land.

My early drawings of the tower showed that the building would need to be five storeys high if the process were to flow totally without pumps, so we compromised on three floors plus a basement, with pumps to deliver the wort from the lauter tun to the brew kettle, and through the heat-exchanger to the fermenters. Note that I said "lauter tun" and not "mash tun." We decided to follow the big brewery practice of having separate vessels to convert the mash (a mash mixer or cooker) and a lauter tun to separate the wort from the spent grains. This added the cost of an additional vessel but gave us advantages in improving process flow when making several brews in a day. With a steam jacket on the mash mixer, we were able to improve the products by having "upward step" temperature plateaus instead of the single-temperature "infusion mash." Our fermenters (originally six) were all double-brew, 100 BBL cylindro-conicals or unitanks with refrigerant jackets.

This was an ambitious brewery, but perhaps my greatest contribution to its unique design was the concept of vessels with no legs. This came after the architect (no doubt having looked at the vessels in the brewpub) called me to say that, on checking the height of the major brewing vessels and their legs, he calculated that they would barely fit beneath a 12-foot ceiling, so the tower would have to be over 60 feet high. My reply was no, there is another way to do this: the vessels do not *need* legs and can be suspended from the steel-beam floors by strong support rings welded to the tanks around their girth, two-thirds of the way up. This change would leave the inspection manways at a convenient height for the brewer, make working platforms unnecessary and greatly reduce the height of the building.

It was just one of the advantages of designing the brewery and building at the same time.

When your brew size reaches 50 BBL, you are not stirring and raking the mash by hand or manually digging out the spent grains. There are mechanisms designed to do this, but they must be incorporated during construction. Neither are you dealing with bagged malt: a bulk system must be installed with a large grain tank and a set-up that delivers the malt to the mill on the uppermost floor. This equipment is expensive, but it eventually pays for itself in reduced man-hours and economies of scale; bulk malt is significantly cheaper than bagged malt.

I sent the drawings to four fabricators including Ripley Stainless, but this time we decided to go with JV Northwest, located just outside Portland. It had a good reputation in small-brewery fabrication and had the advantage of being reasonably close to Bend. The quality of the finished brewing plant justified the decision. And the quality of the products from this big plant was as good, if not improved, from that of the brewpub's products. As well, Deschutes beers were now widely available in bottles.

The brewery came on-stream in 1994. A year earlier, with just the 10 BBL plant, they had sold 7,200 BBL. By 1995 production had reached 30,558 BBL, 76,107 BBL by 1998 and by 2014 sales were a staggering 337,000 BBL.

"You've become a big brewery," I told Gary in 2015.

He laughed. "We never wanted to be a big brewery," he said. "We just wanted to make the best beers around. And look what happened!"

In 1998 they surprised many by opening another brewpub, this one in Portland. Why go to the trouble and expense of having a pub with a brewery in it when they could simply supply it with kegs of beer from Bend?

"Portland is a real hotbed of craft breweries, lots of competition, and it just wouldn't feel right," said Gary. "And besides, we decided the Portland pub would be the place where we tried new recipes and test-marketed them. If they were popular, we might consider making them in the big brewery."

And so today in the Portland pub you can find cask-conditioned beers, real ales aged in oak barrels, fruit-flavoured beers, and other one-off special brews that are not available in Bend. Gary is always thinking of his next move. In 2015 Deschutes beers were sold in twenty-eight US states and the company had three hundred employees.

Amazing.

11 Swans and Yaletown Brewing

MICHAEL WILLIAMS, THE CREATOR OF SWANS HOTEL &
Brewpub in Victoria, was a remarkable man. He had been a
sheep farmer in the English countryside near Wales before
immigrating to Canada in the 1950s. He went to work on
a sheep farm in the BC Interior but soon found the lifestyle on Vancouver Island, with its large British population,
more to his liking. For many years he looked after sheep,
trained sheepdogs and kept a kennel and sheep pasture just
outside Victoria. The turning point in his career came when
he got his realtor's licence and started dealing in properties,
particularly old rundown buildings in Victoria's Old Town,
renovating them and then renting them out as apartments
and businesses. His ability to preserve the character of the
old buildings while giving them a contemporary flair resulted in the revival of lower Johnson Street, including the
now popular Market Square, where he became known as
"Mr. Old Town." He was quite a character, and even after
he had acquired considerable wealth, he was still seen in
the annual Victoria Day parade in his shepherd's smock,
herding a small flock of sheep with a couple of dogs.

In the 1980s Michael bought the old Buckerfield's building, built in 1913 as a seed and feed warehouse on the Inner
Harbour. It was long since empty, and he decided to turn it
into a hotel with two floors of guest rooms above and a pub,
two restaurants and a brewery on the ground floor. It was a
massive undertaking. Just gutting the building and preparing it for this transition cost $80,000. Michael wanted to
get John Mitchell—known in Victoria for his involvement
in Spinnakers—to help him with the brewery, but Mitchell
was tied into a "no competition" contract with his former
partners that kept him from starting any new brewpubs in
the city. John told Michael to phone me.

In 1988, when I first set eyes on the building, its potential was obvious. With its massively thick brick walls
and 12-by-12-inch fir beams supporting floors that had
been made by laminating 2-by-12 fir planks together to
take the heavy floor loading of pallets of grain and feed,
it was perfect for a brewery. But what a huge amount of
work lay ahead! Michael had erected a billboard on the old
Buckerfield's building that said, "From this ugly duckling a
beautiful swan will one day emerge," and added pictures of
the ugly duckling and a swan. From this would come his
name for the project.

We started by planning the ground floor. The area for
the brewery was to be at the rear of the building, but there
was no entrance there. The only access was via the "breezeway," a long passageway that ran the length of the building
from Pandora Street. This gave us a problem bringing in
electrical power and placing the brew kettle vent stack,
and once in operation posed more problems like how to
bring in malt supplies and get rid of brewery wastes. (In
Chapter 9, I have discussed how some of these problems

were tackled.) The area was big enough to allow a plant of 18 HL (400 imperial gallons) with three closed fermenters in a separate room and behind this a long cold room at 4°C (39°F) housing eight (eventually sixteen) storage/serving tanks. An ale cellar was built into the basement beneath the pub and set at 7°C (45°F) to supply the "real ale" at the correct temperature via traditional English hand pumps. To get the ales from the cold storage area to the remote ale cellar required a fixed stainless transfer line 74 feet long, which had to be installed while the building was under reconstruction. Eventually a bottling room was added to the end of the cold room. Once again, no filtration of the beer was contemplated, as clarity was to be obtained by fining and settling. Lager-style beers were served from the cold room through regular "beer towers."

The building had some unique features. In the early days, a railroad line ran down the middle of Store Street, and Buckerfield's had its own spur, which ran right into the middle of the building so that carloads of grain from the Prairies could be unloaded out of the rain. A massive freight elevator had carried the grain to the upper floors. All this had to be removed, but Michael kept two huge gear wheels from the winding mechanism and a piece of the rail line, had them polished up and displayed them in the pub as mementoes of the history of the building. He had some personal memories of the building as well because this was where he had come to have his special dog-food recipe prepared for his sheepdogs. And now here he was, the owner, turning the building into what would become an iconic hotel and brewpub. As he became wealthier, Michael became an art collector, and once when I visited his home—a modest house in a magnificent setting, surrounded by the ocean on its own little peninsula—he showed me some of it. There wasn't room to display more than a fraction of the works by Jack Shadbolt, Norval Morrisseau, Cheryl Samuel, Flemming Jorgensen, Jim Gordaneer and others that he owned.

"You need a bigger place to show them," I said.

"I have one in mind," said Michael. "I intend to hang many of them in the hotel restaurant and pub."

"Really?" I said. "But some of these must be worth a lot. Aren't you afraid they might get damaged by the pub crowd?"

Michael was unfazed. "Oh no. We'll price the rowdies out." And so he did, with Swans becoming something of an art gallery, with even the guest rooms displaying original art.

Early in 1989, with the renovations nearing completion and the brewing plant being fabricated (Ripley in Summerland built the brewing plant and Specific Mechanical of Victoria the storage tanks), I started to think about interviewing people for the position of brewer. We ran an ad in the Victoria papers and got about sixty replies, which I narrowed down to ten for interviews. Back then, hardly anybody had brewing experience, since craft brewing was still in its infancy, so the candidates were a varied lot. My best hope was a college graduate in the sciences. One young fellow who I interviewed I liked immediately. His name was Sean Hoyne, and he had a degree all right, but it was in English. He had also done some science courses and was wondering where his career was leading since he didn't feel he was cut out to be an English teacher and was currently working as an ironworker, erecting rebar structures on building sites. Then he told me he had been experimenting with home brewing and surprised me by producing a couple of bottles of his own beer. (Future interviewees take note: he was the only applicant to do so.)

"I thought you might like to try one of these," he said. I produced some glasses and we cracked the caps.

"We can both try them right now," I said, "and have a talk about them." The first sip was a revelation. "This is a wonderful all-grain beer, no shortcuts, no sugar, a pronounced hop," I said. "Exactly what we want at Swans!"

Sean looked pleased.

"You told me you and your wife live in a one-bedroom apartment," I said. "How do you manage to produce a beer like this in a small apartment?"

"With a great deal of difficulty!" he replied.

We laughed. We had a long talk about beer and brewing, and when Sean left, I was thinking, if this guy has the skills and dedication to make an honest, beautiful beer like that in his apartment, what will he be able to do when he gets his hands on this state-of-the-art brewery I am creating for him? When I next saw Michael Williams, I said, "I think I have found your brewer, one who will make beers you'll be proud of."

So began a long friendship with Sean, one of the very best of the two dozen or so brewers I have trained. He really did forge himself a new career and a successful business. After years with Swans, he was the brewer at the nearby Canoe Club for fourteen years, then took the plunge and started up his own brewery—Hoyne Brewing. His line of original recipes with poetic allusions—Hoyner Pilsner, Dark Matter, Devil's Dream, and how about Gratitude for a Christmas ale?—brewed with high-quality imported ingredients has seen his sales boom, so that within three years he had to buy a new brewing plant, tripling his brew size from 10 to 30 HL and making three brews a day to keep up with demand. He has created jobs for an enthusiastic crew of a dozen young people, and the expanded brewery is just humming. The introductions he writes for his beer labels are gems. Here's one from his Pilsner label:

> On the third night, I handed my sweetie a tall, slender Pilsner, perfectly poured. While holding it up and gazing either at it, or through it at me, she said softly, "You are so fine to me." It was hard to tell if she meant to be heard. "Ambiguity, thy name is Woman," I nearly uttered. Whether she was speaking to me, or to the beer, it was merely semantics. The deal was sealed. I would make it my life's work to make fine beer.

How about charming your partner with *that* over a delicious brew? Go, Sean! You deserve your success.

At Swans the upstairs guest suites were finished before the ground-floor pub, restaurant and brewery area, and I occupied one of those suites for months while overseeing the reconstruction for the brewery installation. I didn't mind "living above the job," as it meant I was instantly available as needed but still had my own room to escape to. But having a comfortable apartment three floors above Store Street and the Johnson Street Bridge, a favourite hangout of the down and out, was an experience. One Sunday morning I awoke to the tormented shouts of some poor soul who was slamming a two-by-four against the front door of the Janion Building across Store Street from Buckerfield's. The Janion dated from the 1890s and had been deserted for a half-century. What did he think he was doing? Should I go down there and talk to him? (Don't get involved!) Should I call the cops? (What will they do with this poor fragment of humanity?) People like the man with the two-by-four had been there for years and years before Michael Williams began gentrifying the neighbourhood. And they still are. Michael, acknowledging that Swans had "priced them out" of the neighbourhood, spent quite a bit of money getting a 40-foot shipping container fitted out with bunks, a cookstove and a privy, then had it placed on the beach close to the bridge for all to use. Later there was a fire in the unit and it was abandoned, with Michael getting a bill from the federal government for removal of the container from the foreshore.

Meanwhile, the brewery project moved on. As we had room for a generous-sized laboratory and a little office, I brought my 1000x microscope from home and started to teach Sean the microbiology of brewing. He just lapped the stuff up. I encouraged his learning by stocking a basic brewing library, the main text being the two-volume *Malting and Brewing Science*, by Hough, Briggs, Stevens and Young, a text that every brewer should have. And I started to think up names and beer styles while formulating the recipes for Swans' basic line of beers: Pandora Pale Ale, Buckerfield's Bitter, Arctic Ale, Appleton Brown Ale, Old Towne Lager. We also brewed seasonal specialties, including a Welsh Spiced Ale for Michael from a recipe I dug out of some brewing archive. It included ginger, coriander and cinnamon, but it wasn't a big seller. Incidentally, Michael had wanted to call his brewery the Swan Brewery, but when he learned that the Swan Brewery in Australia held the worldwide copyright on the name, he settled for the Buckerfields Brewery.

The brewpub opened in 1989 with a blast from a Scots pipe band that deafened everyone, and it has been a great success from day one. As beer writer Joe Wiebe put it in *Craft Beer Revolution*, "the big main bar room with its high ceilings, bricks and beams, and original artwork every-where...I thought Swans was the best place to drink a beer in BC." Well, we probably had to share that honour with Spinnakers, which was only about a mile away at the end of a new walkway the city had created along the water-front. When these two iconic brewpubs were on the draw-ing board, the area between them had been an old, rusty tank farm, built to store fuel for the ships of World War II. Today the rusty tanks are all gone, replaced by condos and a four-star hotel, so that the paved trail with Swans at one end and Spinnakers at the other must be one of the most attractive pub crawls in the world!

We added a small bottling plant in 1992, filling 650-millilitre bottles and selling them at the cold beer and wine store that had been added to the hotel/brewpub com-plex. These days Swans bottled beers are also available at a number of Victoria liquor stores. When Andrew Tessier took over the brewer's job in 2003, he introduced a new line of innovative beer styles that have won twenty-one Canadian brewing awards—ten gold medals, seven silvers and four bronzes—in eleven different categories. Andrew is another wonderfully creative artist in brewing.

Michael Williams lived to see his great vision become an outstanding success—but not much longer. He died of a heart attack while flying to England in 2000, aged just seventy. He had never married or had a family, and when he died, he did what he told me he would do: he left Swans to the University of Victoria. What a guy.

*

Not long before I left Buckerfields Brewery in Sean's capable hands, I was checking the brew runoff when I saw I was being watched by three men in suits through the breezeway window. One of them beckoned to me, and I stepped outside. The youngest of them was Mark James, the oldest his father and the third was Mark's architect. Mark explained that he had acquired a building very similar to the one we were standing in, in the old warehouse area called Yaletown in downtown Vancouver, and he intended to turn it into a brewpub. Was I available to "join the team" as consultant? I told them to go into the pub, sample some beers, and I would join them shortly.

Over beers I learned that Mark wasn't particularly interested in brewing—it was just that he had seen a new and unique business opportunity: brewpubs! His father was a men's tailor on Broadway, and Mark had opened a high-end clothing store up the street from him at Bayswater. Later he had enlarged the business to include a restaurant, Fiasco, which didn't make it in fine dining, so he had turned it into a beer-and-pizza parlour. This had been more successful, but what had amazed him was that 40 percent of its profits came from beer sales. When the brewpub thing happened, he decided that maybe this was the future. Mark and his father were very enthusiastic about the beer at Swans and its surroundings and were keen to hire me for their project. Our discussion ended with me saying that I would stop off in Vancouver on my way home to the Kootenays to see the building and discuss possibilities. That meeting would lead to my designing the first of four pub brewery operations for the Mark James Group. The Group's Yaletown Brewing Company would be the first brewpub in Vancouver.

Warehouse buildings on the West Coast were all built pretty much the same in that pre-World War I era: three storeys high with quadruple-thick brick walls supporting massive beams and solid wood floors. Mark's building was almost identical to the Buckerfield's building, and it stood in a similarly rundown area that was ripe for redevelopment into the trendy area that Yaletown has become today. I guess the only thing better than "location, location, location," is "find the location before it's in vogue and before prices rise." But the building came with a hidden price tag: in the previous decade Vancouver had brought in a new "seismic code," and all old buildings being renovated had to be brought up to this standard. Brick buildings are particularly vulnerable to earthquakes, so in order to satisfy the new regulations, a steel I-beam structure with cross-bracing had to be erected inside the brick walls, and this would cost $150,000. Until it was done, we could not start work.

The plan was to have the pub and brewery on the ground floor, offices and storage on the second and rented offices on the third. A sizable room was built on the second floor for malt storage, which meant we could locate the malt mill in the perfect position—directly over the mash tun. We had just one problem: there was no way to get the sacks of malt up there, save bringing in teams of sherpas to carry them up flights of stairs whenever we got a malt delivery. When I talked to Mark about installing a freight elevator, he agreed to the plan, and it turned into a great convenience, as it allowed him to store items for the kitchen and pub on the second floor as well.

As with Swans, there was no natural gas available at the time, so three-phase electricity was the only option for heating the brew kettle. The brew size was 16 HL with four closed fermenters and a large cold room with twenty storage/serving tanks on the same level. Since the building had no basement, a separate ale tank room beneath the pub (as at Swans) was not an option, so English hand pumps were out, but we had some success in achieving different temperatures for the ales and lagers by partitioning the cold room with a heavy plastic curtain.

The original beams were cleaned up by sandblasting, and character was added to the pub with an antique fireplace from Mexico, refurbished cast-iron railings from England, tiles from France and hardwood flooring recovered from an old Victoria hotel. The guest area was divided into pub and restaurant, the latter having its own brick pizza oven. The city also allowed a generous area along the side of the building for a patio, and this became a very popular place to have a meal and a pint in the summer.

After several interviews, Iain Hill was the guy we hired for the brewer position. He had a degree in biochemistry from UVic and had worked at Shaftebury brewery in East Vancouver. He turned out wonderfully well, producing some of his own unique recipes—his Brick and Beam IPA won BC's Beer of the Year award in 2010. One day when I walked into Yaletown Brewing, he had a surprise for me: "Try this!" he said. The foamy, opalescent beer that surged gleefully up in the tall glass was not only replete with aromas of berries and a whiff of Belgian yeast, it was *pink*!

"Raspberry hefeweizen!" said Iain.

I thought, This is great because *I* would not have brewed a beer like this. Fruit beers are not to my palate, and I wouldn't have believed in it, risked it, had faith that such a product would sell—which are, of course, exactly the reasons you would never see a beer like this coming from one of the big breweries. But on a hot summer day it was the perfect pint, a wonderful surging wheat beer, refreshing, not too alcoholic, with a hint of raspberries... Delicious! And *pink*! The public loved it, and 1,600 litres disappeared in a week.

Iain eventually went on to oversee the brewing operations of all four Mark James brewpubs, plus the Red Truck Brewery. He remained with the Mark James Group for nineteen years, after which he left to start his own brewery on Vancouver's East Side.

Mark rented an apartment for me in the West End, within walking distance of the site in Yaletown. This was perfect, since I insisted on being in on the project from the outset; the floor plans and plant designs were mine, and I wanted to see my vision carried out correctly. The concrete floor finishers laughed when I showed up with coffee for them at 10:00 one night, but I was really there to inspect the slope to the drains on the brewery floors. (One quarter-inch to the foot close to the drains, an eighth of an inch thereafter.) Drains are the lower bowels of a brewery (or a house). The cloaca. And they are just as important in a brewery as in an animal.

I built up a friendship with the construction crews and tradesmen on these jobs because I had learned we could resolve problems better between us than separately. We were a team, working toward a common goal. And there were reciprocal benefits to this relationship. At the

Yaletown site the new building code required that all of the upper-floor office windows be removed and replaced by tempered double-paned windows in "seismic quality" frames. The old windows were perfectly good sheets of quarter-inch plate glass and not very old, and the quandary of the construction contractor was how to dispose of all this glass—and soon. It was going into the Dumpster if he couldn't find a taker for it. I thought of the addition I was putting on my house. What a splendid addition to my addition these windows would be! "But where are you going to store them?" he asked. I had an idea: we would put the sheets of glass in the future grain loft, and after the freight elevator was installed, we would take them down to street level and my truck. With the help of Big Eric, a labourer on the construction crew, the plan was executed to perfection and those sheets of plate glass now reveal the parade of wildlife passing by our "great" room—our party and music room.

Mark James stayed in the background during the building of Yaletown Brewing, but he was always there when a decision or cheque was needed. Just before we opened, with the good beer flowing, he told me, "You know, Frank, what I thought might be a problem, something I was out of my depth with, was brewing the beer. Would it really be first-class? But it was not a problem at all. You took care of everything!" And he showed his appreciation by inviting me to Shabbat supper at his home with his father, wife and kids, welcoming me to the Jewish family celebration.

12 The French Connection

ONE DAY IN JULY 1996 WHEN I WAS IN THE YALETOWN brewery talking with Iain Hill about Mark James's upcoming Whistler brewpub, the barman came in to say that a guy in the pub wanted to talk to me. I said I would see him when we were finished, but our discussion took some time, and when I came out, the barman had gone off shift and nobody else could point the guy out. I looked around the pub, but nobody gave me the high sign, so I concluded that he must have left. As I was expected at John Mitchell's place for dinner, I headed out, but I hadn't gone very far when I heard someone calling after me, "Mr. Appleton! Can we talk?"

The fellow was in his mid-twenties and wore jeans, a sports shirt and sneakers, and carried a small backpack. The most striking thing about him was the mass of blond curls, cut short at the sides so that it looked like the head on a good pint of beer.

"Oh, I'm so glad I caught you," he said. "I came all the way from Portland to try and find you. I'm wondering if you could help me and my partners set up a brewpub."

"Where is it?" I asked.

"It's in Lyon…in France," was the reply.

I must admit I was more than a little skeptical. By this time I was used to people who wanted to get me involved in their brewery/brewpub plans. Most were full of enthusiasm but light on money. When they discovered how much these operations cost, plus all the regulatory hoops they would have to jump through, they went away. Now, this young fellow didn't look like he owned more than what was in his backpack, and when he said the brewpub was in Lyon, my disbelief doubled.

"Why there?" I asked.

He explained that his name was Kurt Huffman and that, though he was from Portland, he had been living and studying in France. In Portland, while playing soccer, he had met Christophe Fargier, who was visiting the States from Lyon on a six-month work permit. Christophe had found work in one of Portland's booming craft breweries, liked what he saw, and had decided to do the same thing back in his hometown, where the number of breweries of any kind numbered zero. He had gathered a group of friends from university (all from well-to-do families) to form a partnership to create a large brewpub. They were looking for a site, Kurt explained. Would I help them once they had found one? He wanted me to go back to the pub with him, have a meal and a pint and talk over the project, but I explained that I was expected at the Mitchells' for dinner.

"Well, can I give you a call in a few months, when we are ready to start?" he asked.

"Sure," I said, giving him my card and thinking I would likely never see or hear from this guy again.

In September, I was installing the plate glass salvaged from Yaletown Brewing in my house addition when I got a call from Kurt. As there had been no communication since our impromptu meeting on the sidewalk, I was a bit surprised.

"Where are you?" I asked.

"Oh, I'm back in Lyon," he said. "We have our site and we're wondering what we have to do to get you started on the project."

Still in a state of disbelief, I told him to send me floor plans of the building and a deposit cheque against my future fees. I had a short conversation with Christophe—who spoke English fluently—and he said he thought 20 HL would be a good size for the plant. When I remarked that this was ambitious, he explained there were no restrictions on selling keg beer to other outlets as well as in their sizable pub. His experience in Portland had taught him a thing or two, like not starting too small and having to buy a larger plant a year or two later when things started booming.

Christophe was a smart businessman. The 1998 World Cup was to be held in France, and one of the venues would be in Lyon. The brand-new stadium being built for it there would become the home of French professional soccer team Olympique Lyonnais after the World Cup, and the pub site Christophe had chosen was about 100 metres from that stadium. Not only that, the city was adding a new metro line station to service the stadium crowds, and that station was right next door to the pub site. This was the perfect case of finding the location before it gets discovered.

The floor plans and cheque arrived, and I settled down to figure out the layout and prepare the vessel and equipment drawings, but I still had a feeling of unreality about the project. Here I was, designing a plant for faraway Lyon, never having seen the site or met any of the partners apart from a five-minute chat with Kurt on the street outside Yaletown Brewing. But the information kept flowing back and forth, and I gradually realized that this thing was going to happen. The building Christophe had found was a warehouse or light industrial unit, a large empty space on one level, and the plan was to divide it with a windowed wall—the brewery on one side and the pub on the other. I could plan the brewery area however I saw fit. Since we had decided to go with steam (fired with natural gas) as the heat source for the kettle, I put the steam plant, refrigeration compressors and other units in a separate mechanical room. This equipment would be purchased in Lyon.

But who was going to build my brewing plant? I thought that in a big city like Lyon, there would certainly be stainless fabricators who could do the work, and when I finished the set of plant drawings and specs, I sent them off to Christophe with instructions to circulate them to likely fabricators. The results were disappointing. Most stainless specialists there were involved in different types of work and refused to bid on the brewery. We did get one bid, but it was unbelievably high—my introduction to how expensive things were in France. I had also sent a set of drawings to Ripley Stainless for a quote more or less as a price check, since I never thought Ed Ripley would have a chance at getting the contract, what with the cost of shipping the plant to France in three 40-foot containers adding more than $20,000 to the price. But that's exactly what happened. After a month of getting nowhere trying to find a French outfit to build the plant at a reasonable price and even contacting fabricators in

England and the US, I got the go-ahead from Christophe: "Have Ripley build it."

There were some very positive aspects to this arrangement: I could drive over to Summerland and check the work as it progressed, there were no language problems, and because Ripley and I had worked together on so many jobs, I knew there would be no unpleasant surprises when I had to assemble the plant in Lyon. But the lack of stainless suppliers and competent TIG welders in France made me realize that I couldn't rely on much local backup. I had to have *everything* in those containers when they left Ripley, right down to the last nut and bolt. I examined my lists of equipment over and over to be sure I wasn't missing anything. It proved to be worth it when it came time to hook up the plant.

I decided that the brewing plant should be a two-vessel system, which is useful if you are only heating the brew kettle but still want the ability to have upward-step temperature rises during mash conversion, which is what Christophe wanted. In this system the mash is made up in the kettle with steam applied to raise its temperature through conversion. Then the whole of the mash is run by gravity into the lauter tun, which has slotted plates in the bottom to separate the sweet wort from the spent mash. The wort is then pumped back to the kettle for boiling with the hops. For this to work, the kettle must be raised so it drains by gravity into the lauter tun, which meant that a tubular steel support structure with an elevated walkway and spiral stair access had to be built around the kettle. This was all constructed and assembled in Ripley's shop. The vessels were arranged around the shop floor in the exact positions they would have in the brewpub, and the considerable amount of fixed pipework needed to connect them was then precision-welded in place. Afterward, it was all dismantled and put into the containers. The parts numbered in the hundreds, right down to the stainless shims that would be needed to level the vessels.

I arrived in Lyon in early July 1997, a day ahead of the brewing plant, and met the project partners. All were in their late twenties, and each one had a specific role in bringing the brewpub into being. It was a fun group to work with. Christophe, who was a business graduate, had prepared a workflow chart to show which jobs were to be tackled and when, so the whole thing was coordinated to come together smoothly and brewing to start in early August. It was important to keep to this schedule, since I had only allotted myself two months before I had to return home. The first thing was to be ready for the arrival of the containers, take everything out and move the vessels into their places. Christophe told me he had already contacted a company that moved large, heavy objects, as we had to empty the containers within one day or we would be liable for demurrage charges if we ran overtime.

"How much did they quote to do the job?" I asked. His reply was staggering—it was the equivalent of $7,000! "That's outrageous!" I said. "Do you know of a tool rental shop, something that has pallet jacks, dollies, chain hoists, come-alongs, floor jacks…that kind of thing?"

"For sure," he replied.

"And do you have some friends, guys who might give us a hand tomorrow?"

"Friends?" said Christophe. "We're building a brewery— do we have friends! I can get you a whole soccer team!"

"Right, then," I said. "Phone around, get them down here in the morning, and let's go find that tool rental shop."

The brewery building had a loading dock exactly the right height, which was a great help. And Ripley had provided cradles of Styrofoam and plywood to support each of the vessels, which had been laid on their sides to fit into the containers. I knew that if we could slip a couple of pallet jacks, fore and aft, under these cradles we could push the vessels out of the containers as sweetly as they had gone in. The small stuff could be wheeled in on dollies or carried in by the guys. As it happened, the only tricky bit came when we were standing the big tanks upright, but the building was of open steel-beam joist construction and we managed to hang a chain from one beam with a chain hoist attached to lift them up. The containers were emptied and the vessels placed in position by mid-afternoon, and we didn't get charged a cent of demurrage. The total cost was about $500 for the tool rental and some cases of beer for the boys. Christophe was overjoyed: "Monsieur Appleton is great! Just great!"

Over the next few days I connected the fixed pipework while our building construction crew assembled the brew kettle platform. The plant was now ready to be hooked up to the electrical, steam and water systems. We were off to a flying start, but there were roadblocks ahead: the journeymen electricians, steamfitters and plumbers were *unbelievably* slow. They were being paid by the hour, so what did they care? Sometimes they wouldn't show up at all, as their boss had had them go to another job. At first I wasn't too bothered, since I was busy ordering malt and hops, starting a yeast culture and locating other items that we needed. But as the weeks went by and we still had no services to the plant, I got a little incensed.

I was just not used to the work ethic (or lack of one) in France, especially at the height of summer, when every French worker feels it is their unquestionable right to down tools and take the family to the seaside or country for a month. I got asked several times why we were building this brewery in midsummer, when everybody in France goes *en vacances*. Attitudes were just more laid-back in France. While it is not a bad way to live, it's hell if you have a job to do and a deadline to work to. Hour-and-a-half lunch-times were the norm, and some of our workers thought nothing of bringing a bottle of wine in their lunch pail and emptying it by quitting time. The best of the workers was Pasquale, who would tackle any job, including climbing tall ladders to install vent stacks and other things that went out the roof. I told him one day I didn't want to see him atop a ladder after he had downed a bottle of wine, but he just smiled sweetly and said that wine didn't make him drunk—it just made him *bon*.

Then briefly we were swept up in our own *vacance*. My partner, Jean, flew in the day before Bastille Day, and Christophe's father gave the brewery partners and their guests use of his country house in the Ardèche for the weekend. Jean and I and the five young friends got into two little cars and headed at top speed south on the crowded freeway toward the Mediterranean. Halfway there we made a sharp exit and headed into this rough country, hilly with ancient volcanoes, which reminded me of the interior of southern California. This was where Christophe's father, a surgeon, had purchased a classic, hundred-year-old French country manor and was slowly making improvements to the property, including the installation of a good-sized swimming pool. It gets very hot and dry in the Ardèche in summer, so we spent most of our time outdoors by the barbecue or the pool. A partner I had not yet met, Vincent, arrived a few hours late, and Christophe, Kurt and Bernard immediately jumped up with a yell, grabbed him and threw him, kicking and screaming and fully clothed, into the pool. I never did figure out what this greeting meant, but it convinced me that I was involved with a close-knit bunch of guys who knew both how to work and how to have a good time together.

Back in Lyon the work to get the plant running dragged on. We just could not get the tradesmen to go any faster. If I stood and watched an electrician or plumber at work, he went even slower, sometimes downing his tools and staring back at me. With the end of July approaching, my patience was wearing thin.

"This is crazy," I said to Christophe. "This work should have been completed in two weeks easily."

"What do you think we should do?" he asked.

"I know what I would do if we were in Canada," I said. "I would tell their crew boss if they couldn't get the plant ready for brewing by the end of July, he should fire them all and get in another crew."

Christophe was alarmed. "Oh no! You can't do that! We would never be able to get another crew. I had a hard enough time finding *anyone* who was willing to work at *vacance* time. If you talk to them like that, they will quit and then we will be in real trouble."

"Well, it's up to you," I said. "Right now we have all the materials on site, I've prepared the recipes, have a yeast culture growing in our starter fermenter, and you're paying me to stand around fuming because we can't get brewing."

Poor Christophe was at a loss. I came up with a suggestion: Why didn't Jean and I go on our own little *vacance* for a week, which they wouldn't have to pay me for; with me out of the way, hovering, maybe Christophe could get through to these guys and get them motivated. He agreed, and Jean and I took a train to the south of France. We visited Avignon, Nîmes and Arles, then headed for the Mediterranean through the Camargue, a semi-wild, flat expanse in the Rhône delta. Here wild white horses and wild boar roam amid tens of thousands of birds, including migrating flamingos. Reaching the sea, we found a lovely little seaside town called Saintes-Maries-de-la-Mer, a sleepy, relaxed place, nothing like the bustling, expensive French Riviera, and we spent the rest of our week there. As the town is only a few hours' drive from the Spanish border, one of the attractions was mock bullfights. A couple of bulls with wreaths of braided flowers around their horns were let loose in the ring, and a half-dozen young guys tried to pluck a wreath off the horns while others distracted the bull. You needed to be nimble and brave (or foolhardy) to try this.

As we headed back to Lyon, I wondered what we would find at the brewery. But there was good news on that front. The plant still wasn't ready to go, but it was almost there. What surprised me most was the increased number of journeymen on the job, including the boss of the steamfitting/plumbing company, who had his sleeves rolled up and was threading iron pipe.

"What did you say to them?" I asked Christophe.

He smiled. "I told them that you had to leave at the end of the month, and if we didn't have you to take us through the first few brews, it would be a disaster." He pointed to the starter fermenter, which had been fizzing merrily away.

Now it was quiet, having fermented out. "I told them this special yeast was ready to go, and if it was not used by this week, it would die and we would not be able to brew. We would have no beer to open the pub, the business would fold before it even started, and they would not get paid." A very French solution to the problem!

The plant was ready for the first brews by the end of the week. We had three weeks left.

*

Christophe had decided to call the pub "Ninkasi Ale House," with a logo featuring what looked to me like an Egyptian-style female eye.

"Wherever did you come up with the name?" I asked.

Christophe looked surprised. "You don't know? I thought everyone in brewing knows Ninkasi. She was the Sumerian goddess of beer!"

Well, it just goes to show you never stop learning, and I am still learning about beer, even from brewers I am training. Ninkasi, my research showed, was indeed revered as the Sumerian goddess of beer—and of alcohol and pure water too—and the Hymn to Ninkasi, circa 1800 BC, is the oldest written record of how beer used to be brewed by making a mash of *bappir* bread, adding honey and dates, fermenting it, then drinking the brew through straws. This text is also important because it shows that brewing beer was the responsibility of women, and that they guarded the secrets of successful brewing. Women remained in charge of brewing for millennia, until men realized the importance of beer, which was said to "satisfy the desire" and "sate the heart." No drunken rowdies here!

One of the most interesting things about the Ninkasi partners was that only one of them owned a car, and although public transit via the metro and buses was good, they all found bikes to be the cheapest and best way to get around the congested city. They had found an apartment for me in one of the university's student residences, now almost empty for the summer, but it was about three kilometres from Gerland, the area of Lyon where the brewery was located, so Christophe asked if I preferred to have a bus/metro pass or a bike to get to work. The weather was beautiful so I opted for a bike, and we went to a nearby second-hand store and found a mountain bike model for a reasonable price. The next morning I pedalled off to the site via a shortcut and found I could get there in fifteen minutes, compared to a half-hour by the more circuitous metro/bus route. Great! I stowed my bike inside the brewery building and started work. At lunchtime Christophe asked me to join him at a favourite local bistro. Off we went on foot for the usual unhurried "lunch hour," and when we returned, my bike was gone! Since I had left it in the building, I figured someone had moved it, but no—it had been stolen. The large loading-bay doors had been left open, and someone had snuck in and taken it when most of us were literally "out to lunch." It was the first day I'd had it! The bicycle thieves in Lyon were notorious. You couldn't take your eyes off your bike or it would be gone. Kurt had his stolen—again from inside the building—one evening when he and Christophe were actually there working late. They caught sight of the thief as he pedalled away and Christophe gave chase, but to no avail.

Despite the bike thieves and the slow workmen, Lyon had a lot of charm. As it sits at the confluence of the Rhône and Saône rivers, it has been an important crossroads since Roman times and there are Roman ruins throughout the city, particularly on the hill called Fourvière, which dominates the city. While we were there, Joan Baez headlined a concert in the restored Roman amphitheatre, and Jean and I went. We were a bit late arriving, and every place in the stone seating area was taken, but we found a section of Roman column above the rim of the theatre that we could sit on. At that distance above the stage, Baez was a tiny figure in a blue spotlight, but the sound was good and we had an incredible view over the city as the sun set. For some reason, the required finish on the outside of buildings in Lyon is a brick-red stucco, and the whole city glowed pink in the sunset—an unforgettable sight. (Maybe that's the reason for the brick-red finish.)

The Ninkasi brewing plant performed well, and we managed to rush a brew through for the opening party, just two days before I had to return to Canada. There was a good crowd of the partners' friends and relatives, and John and Jenny Mitchell came from England, where they were visiting relatives. We even had a pickup band—ourselves. When we were in the Ardèche, I had discovered Vincent was quite the musician, able to play guitar and drums, he discovered I knew a lot of Beatles songs, and we combined with two other guys to form a band. It was a fun send-off, and a great relief that we had the plant running before I had to go. The brewery was in good hands with Christophe—the experience he had gained working at the brewery in Portland would now pay off.

Ninkasi was a great success in this land of wine, coming on-stream a year before the World Cup came to Lyon, when the place was packed with thirsty soccer fans every day. They sold 220 HL of beer out of the pub during the tournament. And to top it off, France won the final and hoisted the cup. Christophe later wrote me, "We haven't seen a time like this in France since World War II ended."

Today Ninkasi regularly welcomes big-name bands from across Europe, as it's large enough to hold 150 fans with no problem. It is also listed in a number of guidebooks as one of the most important places to visit in Lyon. Some of the original partners have moved on, but Christophe Fargier is still the *grand patron* of his creation.

Sea to Sky

IN 1995 I DESIGNED AND INSTALLED THE BREWERY FOR Tin Whistle Brewing in Penticton, and as the project was winding down, Mark James announced that he had acquired a lot in the village at Whistler, where he would build his second brewpub, and he invited me to come on board as the brewing consultant. When I had skied at Whistler in the late 1960s, the "village" had not even existed, and the spot where Mark was now planning to build his brewpub had been the town dump! How times had changed.

Meanwhile a brewpub plus a twenty-room hotel and a restaurant were in the works in Squamish, halfway between Vancouver and Whistler. An old logging town, Squamish was reinventing itself as an outdoor playground with opportunities for skiing, rock climbing, boating and kayaking. The Howe Sound Inn and Brewpub was the project of partners Dave Fenn and Stephen Shard; having admired the Horseshoe Bay Brewery and Spinnakers, they had asked John Mitchell to advise them on the design of their brewery and pub. John in turn asked me to be around for the start-up. In 1996 the project was well underway when Mark James stopped by to check it out on his way back from Whistler. I asked him what was happening in Whistler. "Well," he joked, "we just went up there to inspect our million-dollar hole in the ground."

The Howe Sound Inn was in a class of its own compared to the other hotels in Squamish, with its high ceilings and big exposed beams, a range of beers served via hand pumps or towers—your preference—and a large selection of pub and restaurant food. It was outstanding, but trade was slow in the early years. It should have been the perfect stop-off for the skiing set. The trouble was, the Sea to Sky Highway doesn't go *through* Squamish, it goes past it, and so did all the well-heeled skiers who were eager to get to the slopes or get home. When I skied at Whistler between 1966 and 1972, I don't think I ever stopped at Squamish unless I needed gas. Certainly, driving that dangerous highway in winter, the last thing I needed was to stop and have a couple of pints on the way home. In addition, although Fenn and Shard's inn was on the main street, it was at the farthest end of town from the highway. And while the site should have been idyllic, as it overlooked tidewater and had a commanding view of Howe Sound, the view also included a log dump, the place where the logging trucks emerging from the rain forest on the slopes of the picture-perfect mountains dumped their logs into the ocean. And to the southwest, plumes of smoke rose from the stacks of the recently upgraded Woodfibre pulp mill, owned by Western Forest Products. Ah, the contradictions of British Columbia. Some of the most staggeringly beautiful mountain scenery in the world, but when you get back to ground level, you find it dominated by industries like logging and mining.

Things were very slow at the Howe Sound Inn and Brewpub for a number of years. Stephen Shard left the partnership, and Dave Fenn and his sister Leslie, backed by their family, struggled to make a profit. Then slowly things began to turn around. With property values and rents in Vancouver sky-high, people began to see Squamish, just forty-five minutes by car from the city, as a bedroom community. As well, with the new high-end hotels in Whistler came high room rates, and skiers began to look to Squamish as a reasonable alternative. Best of all, however, in 2001 the provincial government eased its stingy liquor laws to allow brewpubs to sell their beer to other outlets, and this change really turned things around for the operation. Howe Sound Brewing began selling kegs of beer to pubs in Vancouver, then got into bottling, choosing one-litre bottles with a "pot stopper" (Grolsch-style) closure because they are easier to fill. This turned into a smart decision because its bottles are noticeably different from those of the other craft breweries, most of which use 650-millilitre crimp-cap bottles. What I like about these big bottles is that you can share one with friends or reseal it, so if you are not into downing a whole litre, you can put it back in the fridge and enjoy the rest later. They are also the home brewer's perfect container.

Many of the original beers at Howe Sound Brewing were John Mitchell's recipes and bore his name, but since 2002 when I trained Franco Corno to take over the brewing duties, he has come up with many creative styles of his own, such as King Heffy Imperial Hefeweizen, Pumpkineater Imperial Pumpkin Ale and Total Eclipse of the Hop IPA. They all have colourful labels and an amusing promotional style. During the financial crisis of 2008, Dave and his crew wondered how to bring a little humour to a grim outlook, and they brewed a beer called Bailout Bitter with a graph on the label showing the financial market's steep downward curve. The story hit the local papers and was then picked up by news outlets across the country. In 2010 when they wanted to produce something related to the Winter Olympics taking place in Whistler and Vancouver, they were up against the proscriptions the International Olympic Committee imposed on the use of the Olympic rings or medals for unlicensed promotions. They came up with Three Beavers Imperial Red Ale, and the label showed beavers wearing gold, silver and bronze medals. But the IOC couldn't come after them, since the medals were those won by Howe Sound beers in international competitions. Smart.

I am happy to say that both John Mitchell's and my own name appear on Howe Sound's labels as "brewpub pioneers" who have been involved in their operation. My input has been quite small, mainly consisting of being readily available to sort out problems and train brewers. When there are problems with the brewing, Dave Fenn will phone John, and John usually says, "Phone Frank." Such was the case in 2002 when the brewer abruptly walked out, leaving no backup person who knew how to brew and a brewery woefully in need of a thorough cleaning. That's when Franco Corno volunteered as a trainee brewer, and together we cleaned up the mouldy grist in the grist hopper, scrubbed the dirty tanks and dirty beer lines, and overhauled the aging steam boiler. It took a week to get things clean and ready to brew again, and though it was some initiation for Franco, he received a great lesson in how not to run a brewery. Since he took over, I have had no emergency calls from Dave. In fact, Franco was in charge during the replacement of the original plant with one three times the size, and Howe Sound is now brewing two shifts a day. Things are looking good at last—talk about dogged perseverance on the part of Dave, Leslie and Franco.

Having been given the freedom to design the brewery while the building was at the drawing-board stage, John had done a great job, placing the grain loft and malt mill on the floor above the brewhouse, the brewing and fermentation on the ground floor, and cold storage for aging and serving tanks in the basement. A small steam plant, which heated the brew kettle and mash tun, was also down there. (Today the basement contains added closed fermenters and the bottle filling and kegging operations.) A neat spiral staircase connects the levels.

One thing I did not care for in this set-up, however, was the little hop back that John had designed for hop removal. It was like the one we had used in Horseshoe Bay, but it was far too small to contain the amount of spent hops left in the brew, so most of the hop and trub sludge stayed in the almost-flat bottom of the kettle. The only way to remove the spent hops was for some poor devil to climb into the kettle and shovel the hot sludge into buckets, which were then passed out the manway to someone else for disposal. It was a horrible, sweaty, time-consuming job—for which there was an easy answer. When I got the call in 2002 to rehabilitate the operation, I thought, Enough of this! I figured that the kettle, with its squat dimensions and almost-flat bottom, could double as a whirlpool tank, and I decided we should switch from whole hops to pellets because they dissolve into a very fine debris in the boil. When the brew is rotated inside the tank by pump action, then left for 50 to 90 minutes to rest, the pellet debris and the sludge are deposited in the centre of the tank, where they can easily be hosed out after the clarified wort is drawn off. We didn't have the pipework set-up to do this but we experimented, stirring the brew with a long canoe paddle to get enough rotation to test my idea out. It worked like a charm. We ran the brew off after the spinning and settling, and the sludge flushed out easily. No more climbing into the tank for a half-hour of shovelling in the steamy, smelly heat. Franco and Dave loved it, and the only negative feedback I got was from John. Introducing pellets was anathema to John (who had never climbed into that kettle to clean out the spent hops), and though there were no negative effects on the beer flavour, he believes it is just "not the way brewing should be done." Although he now looks upon me as a "pellet man," I hasten to say that I have designed several breweries that do use whole hops, but these breweries were specifically designed for them, with a steep slope on the kettle bottom cone, a 4- or 6-inch outlet and a large hop back that will take the hops from an entire brew.

All this is academic now, of course, since business for Howe Sound Brewing boomed after the relaxation of the liquor laws that allowed them to sell beer by the keg to other pubs that were crying out for high-quality craft beers and sell bottled beer in BC Liquor Stores. Hallelujah! The granting of the 2010 Winter Olympics to Whistler and Vancouver, and the consequent reconstruction of the Sea to Sky Highway along Howe Sound's perilous shoreline vastly improved Howe Sound Brewing's situation, and in response the Fenn family replaced the brewery's 10 HL brewing system with a 20 HL brewhouse (using hop pellets in a kettle/whirlpool), more fermenters and more tanks for products in cold storage. Sales responded phenomenally again after the laws preventing beer sales between provinces and into the United States were struck from the books. In the first ten years of operation (1996–2006) they brewed 1,000 brews of 10 HL, or 10,000 HL. In the next eight years (2006–2014), they produced 8,000 brews of 20 HL, or 160,000 HL. They are now brewing twice a day seven days a week, and Franco, once the lone brewer, has a staff of twelve. The plant contains eight 20 HL fermenters, three 80 HL conditioning tanks, five 80 HL bright beer tanks and two dozen of the old 10 HL tanks, useful for specialty beers. They have added a canning line to the bottling operation, with their lager the big seller in cans. It took a long while and the realization on the part of the BC government that craft beer was actually good for people, good for business and good for the province, but good beer has finally prevailed.

Today Howe Sound's beer sales are zooming, with products in stores as far away as Ontario and into the States. Things look rosy at home base in Squamish for the hotel and the pub too. The Britannia Beach copper mine, which poured its poisonous effluent into the Sound for a half-century, closed in 1974, and by 2008 the pollution flowing into Britannia Creek from the old mine had been cut by 98 percent. The Woodfibre mill, a similar producer of massive air and water pollution, was closed and dismantled in 2006 and the log dump closed soon after. The herring are returning to the Sound, and pink salmon are coming back to the creeks to spawn. The seals and orcas that feed on this bounty are being sighted in Howe Sound for the first time in recent memory. However, the hotel and pub face a new threat promoted by the BC government:

a liquefied natural gas (LNG) terminal at the site of the old pulp mill, a mere ten kilometres from Squamish. The dangers of an explosion and fire at this type of installation are such that in the States LNG facilities are legislated to remote locations. Situating an LNG plant in a narrow waterway with roughly 10,000 people living on its shores wouldn't even be considered there. In BC and Canada no such legislation exists.

*

The High Mountain Brewhouse in Whistler was quite a different operation from Howe Sound Brewing. Mark James had created a limited partnership, the Mark James Group, and the company had no qualms about spending $5 million or so to make Whistler's first brewpub a hit. With its strategic location in the heart of the new village and the Winter Olympics on the way, it was sure to succeed. The building was something of an architect's dream with a huge pub on two levels, a massive stone fireplace, pool tables and even a clock tower, but it was a brewer's conundrum, as the architect had never designed a brewpub before and his attitude seemed to be, "This is the space allotted for the brewery. Make it work." The brewery space was in a glass enclosure above the ground-floor kitchen and pub. It wasn't quite a goldfish bowl setting but pretty close. The main problem was the limited amount of space to accommodate all the equipment needed for a 16 HL brewery. I did away with a separate whirlpool tank by incorporating it into a combined kettle/whirlpool. I had designed the brewery to run on steam from a small boiler in a room below it on the main floor, but when the kitchen took up all of that space, the architect decided the boiler had to be located *in* the brewhouse. In this crowded space, the crew had built a large cupboard to hide the boiler from view but ignored the building code, which said there should be at least two feet of space between the boiler unit and the closest wall to allow for inspection and maintenance. This would lead to problems later. And after construction was well underway, Mark directed me to enlarge the plant from 16 to 20 HL. This was a case of "If the shoes are too tight, make the feet fit," which can drive you crazy if you are the guy who has to walk in those shoes.

And then there was the cold room/cellar, which was at the pub level and visible from an area containing a pool table. It was designed to hold sixteen 16 HL tanks with reasonable space to work between them. Then Mark wanted 20 HL tanks and at the same time someone decided a second pool table was necessary—and the cellar area was reduced accordingly. The result was that the tanks were squeezed into this tight space, and the fixed pipework all had to be cut off and repositioned. We ended up with a room that the poor brewers who have to work there call "the submarine room," as they are liable to get banged heads and elbows as they work.

Another problem for me was how to get the malt up to the third-floor mill room above the brewhouse, and how to get the bins of spent grains out. In the end I did make it work, but it took a lot of my time redrawing the plans and changing equipment and a lot of Mark's money to accomplish what was required. The mill room was tiny with just enough space for the mill and a few sacks of specialty malt, so storing large amounts of basic pale malt there was out of the question. There was a suitably large area next to the mill room, but Mark had reserved this for a guest suite. After some pondering, I decided there was just no way to accommodate bagged pale malt. The alternative was a bulk grain tank outside the building with a delivery system to bring the malt to the mill room. This would usually have been accomplished with a grain auger, but the run from the grain tank to the mill room was 180 feet with a vertical rise of 30 feet within the building; an auger was out of the question. The only alternative was a pneumatic system that would blow the grain through a pipe to its destination, but it came with a price tag of $10,300, and with the necessary grain silo and digital weighing system, the total cost would be $14,500. On the other hand, a push-button system of this kind would save the brewer from having to lug sacks of malt. Mark agreed to have it installed.

High Mountain's construction went on through the winter of 1996–97, and we opened the following spring. I had pushed for the brewery to be completed first, at least a month before the pub, since lead time would be needed to brew, ferment and age the beer before the opening. This was done, but it meant that the trainee brewer, Ben Schottle, and I were working amid the construction workers and drywallers. At one point I joked that it wouldn't matter if a bit of drywall mud got into the brew, since the mountain spring water of Whistler was so soft that we had to add 150 ppm calcium sulphate, which is also gypsum, when brewing ales. For centuries it had been recognized that beers made in the Burton-on-Trent area of England (Bass for example) were the best in the country, but no one knew why. When analytical chemistry finally came to brewing, chemists examined the water to find out what was in it and found that it was slightly hard—not too hard, like in the area around London, where calcium deposits in kettles and boiler pipes cause problems—but about 250 ppm dissolved calcium. It has a subtle but important reaction in the wort, improving the extraction of hop oils, the precipitation of proteins, fermentation and beer flavour. After this discovery was made, brewers began "Burtonizing" soft waters by adding calcium sulphate. Now this is a common practice in areas that have very soft brewing water.

One of the problems with Whistler is that *everything* is more expensive there, especially accommodation, since you have to compete with the affluent skiing set, and brewers can't afford it. So after a couple of years at High Mountain, Ben Schottle moved to Victoria and we had several brewers come and go after that. In 2005 Dave Woodward got the job. A BC boy who had gone to England and put himself through brewing school at the University of Sunderland, Dave came up with some wonderful recipes: Big Wolf Bitter and Woodward's IPA, plus a pink raspberry ale on tap for Gay Pride Week. I will say this for Mark: he allows his brewers to use their creativity in coming up with products. It stimulates customer interest to find fresh, new beers available as "seasonal specials," and it certainly gives satisfaction to the brewer. Unfortunately, Dave also found Whistler too pricey, and he was followed at High Mountain in 2010 by Derrick Franche, formerly a brewer at DIX in Vancouver.

The Brewhouse at Whistler, as it came to be known, was bound to be a hit, as it is the only brewpub around and it's in a central location in the midst of the action. It has a see-through log fireplace for winter comfort and a huge patio for outdoor summer dining and drinking. Musical acts are featured regularly. The pub is one of the stops on the walking tour of the town. After hitting the big time in 2010 with the Winter Olympics, Whistler has become one of the world's top destination ski resorts.

14 Want to Be a Brewmaster?

Education and training

It is gratifying to see so many young people eager to get into jobs in the craft beer business, and even more gratifying that there are jobs for them. I have trained a couple dozen brewers, and it has been a great experience for me to share my knowledge and see the seeds of it growing into this phenomenon, the craft beer revolution. I could not have imagined anything like this back in 1972 when I walked out of the O'Keefe brewery, dismayed by the seeming end of my career in brewing.

When John Mitchell read my article "The Underground Brewmaster" in 1981, he was a bit lucky in finding a like spirit who was fed up with the bland light lagers that represented 90 percent of the beer market, all made by the Big Three breweries—Molson, Labatt and Carling O'Keefe. People with a background like mine, educated in food science, microbiology and brewing, were largely working for those same Big Three and were not about to jeopardize their positions by helping him make "real ale" for his pub. As he has said many times since then, "If it hadn't been for you, Appleton, who would I have turned to?" A good question. There were several recognized brewing schools in Europe, but just two in the US and none in Canada. The graduates of the Siebel Institute in Chicago and the Brewing School at the University of California at Davis were mostly channelled into jobs with the mega breweries.

Thankfully, that is not the case today. In the past few years, several Canadian post-secondary institutions have responded to the great surge in craft brewing and small-brewery openings by offering brewing courses. In British Columbia, Kwantlen Polytechnic University offers a two-year course at the Langley campus, where they have added a working brewhouse. Simon Fraser University's Faculty of Science lists a two-year Craft Beer and Brewing Essentials certificate course. In Ontario, Niagara College has a two-year diploma course with an optional two years for the degree program. A parallel course is offered at Olds College in Alberta. An added attraction at some colleges is an opportunity to sell the finished product at the college. Great stuff!

I should add that this last idea is hardly new. In 1340, Queen's College, Oxford, appointed a brewer and built a stone and wood brewhouse, 55 by 22 feet, which still stands today and is used to brew a strong ale once a year using medieval methods and aging the product in oak casks for a year. It is served up on special occasions in two-handled silver mugs (loving cups) and passed around "to the great content of the Fellows and Scholars." You can see pictures of this brewery in the opening pages of Volume 1 of H. Lloyd Hind's *Brewing Science and Practice*, the standard

English-language reference text on the subject of brewing for fifty years, which can be viewed at www.hathitrust.org.

It is quite possible to make good beer by rote, following a recipe and a set of procedures that are known to give successful results. I have trained many brewers who didn't have a science background but were good learners on the job. One of the first things I always taught them: be proud of what you do and remember that you are a link in a four-thousand-year-old creative tradition called beer making, much esteemed by humankind. Of course, being proud of what you do is almost impossible if you are a mere cog in a factory cranking out a hundred thousand bottles of bland light beer a day, but if you are lucky enough to work in a small brewery making beers that have the character and individuality your skills gave them, well, there is nothing like it. I tell fledgling brewers to say to themselves, "I am a brewer of beer! I make the drink that makes folk happy!" Nothing compares to getting praise for your products from drinkers who didn't even know your name before downing a pint of your best bitter. It puts you in a class with chefs, artists, winemakers and woodworkers—all those creative people whose mission in life is to make products that please people.

But while a brewer can put a brew through satisfactorily, if you aspire to be a brewmaster, you must understand that this is a unique job that requires a unique person with a unique set of attributes. You must have a sensitive palate. You must have a complete grasp of all aspects of the process, from evaluating raw malt to knowing how to achieve the correct carbonation levels in the finished product. You must have a knowledge of biochemistry (mash conversion, fermentation and aging), physics (carbonation, Boyle's law, pH, specific gravity, refrigeration) and above all microbiology (yeast purity control, tracking down plant infections, checking cleanliness). You must be the kind of person who will keep that stainless-steel plant cleaner than your dishwasher can clean dishes and who will check your procedures by plating out samples of wort, beer, yeast and tank swabs on Petri dishes. You can be relied on to be creative in designing and experimenting with new recipes. You have to put up with the drudgery of cleaning out tanks and beer lines, plus keeping records and filling out the endless forms required for paying different levels of government their taxes (which are far lower in the US). You won't object to staying after hours to see a slow-lautering brew into the fermenter or to take a tour group through the plant. Add to that all the basic maintenance skills a brewmaster needs, and you might wonder if it is possible to find a person with all these attributes. But there is no shortage of applicants. Why? Because the job is an unparalleled opportunity for someone who likes beer to learn the mysteries of the complete brewing process, be creative, and get the direct satisfaction of heartfelt thanks from customers—something that those who work for the major breweries never get.

Cleanliness and sanitation

If "cleanliness is next to godliness," a clean brewery is a temple to good beer. A day's brewing in a small brewery is a physical workout, but a good brewmaster never goes home promising himself, "I'll clean those hoses (tanks, filling machine, spent grain bins, floors) tomorrow." He must leave the place spotless. Sloppy habits reflect a negligent attitude, which will eventually be rewarded with poor quality beer or—worse—a serious infection.

In the brewhouse, cleaning is restricted to removing the spent mash, spent hops and trub from the vessels and cleaning out the residue. Further sanitation is not required, since the next brew through will be boiled in the kettle and spoilage organisms killed. But when the wort is cooled at the heat-exchanger stage and thereafter through fermentation and storage, it is absolutely necessary that the vessels, transfer lines and hose fittings are properly cleaned, because you cannot sanitize that which has not been thoroughly cleaned. Whether you use solutions of alkaline-based sanitizers (sodium hypochlorite or chlorinated trisodium phosphate) or acid-based ones (iodophors or peracetic acid/hydrogen peroxide), sterilizing depends on the strong oxidizing effect of nascent oxygen, which ruptures the protein sheath of micro-organisms and destroys them. However, this strong oxidation is not selective and will combine with any residue left by poor cleaning, quickly depleting the sanitizer. The sanitizer needs time to act—thirty minutes minimum or—better yet—leave it on the walls of vessels or in the lines and hoses until rinsing out just before next use.

Pitching yeast

This is the next hazard for the brewmaster. Yeast is the most likely reservoir of infection in a clean brewery because it is recycled after it has been through a series of previous brews, with chances of picking up contamination each time. Killing spoilage organisms when they are mixed with another living micro-organism such as yeast that must be kept in top shape is a conundrum that has yet to be completely solved. It's like injecting a person with an antibiotic that will kill off a bloodstream infection but also cause death: "The procedure was a success, but unfortunately the patient died." The best way to avoid getting contaminated yeast is the same as for the human example: don't get the disease in the first place. What this means in brewing terms is paying strict attention to cleanliness and aseptic techniques when handling yeast.

Before the invention of heat-exchangers designed to cool the wort after the boil by running it over metal plates with cold water on the other side, the standard method of cooling was to pump the wort into a "coolship"—a large, open, flat copper vessel that would hold an entire brew at a foot deep or less. The coolship was located high up in the brewery, and the walls surrounding it were provided with louvres to allow cool air to waft through. Left there overnight, the wort would cool to a temperature where the yeast could be added without killing it. Nobody thought too much about contamination with airborne micro-organisms since they didn't know about them, and in most areas they got away with this trick. However, the low-lying areas of Flanders, in present-day Belgium, were a different story. This flat, damp country was noted for growing cabbages and other members of the *Brassica* family, and the spoiled cabbage and discarded leaves were left in the fields to rot. The rot was caused by a host of micro-organisms, including some of the worst spoilage organisms in the brewing microbiologist's lexicon: *Brettanomyces, Lactobacillus delbrueckii, Pediococcus damnosus* and others. These tiny mischief-makers were quite happy to get wafted away from rotting cabbage and deposited in warm wort. They didn't even mind coexisting with *Saccharomyces cerevisiae* when the brewing yeast was pitched in, since some of them fed on the alcohol produced. The resultant beer had a strong, variable, acetic/phenolic or "horsey" flavour called Lambeek (today it's known as lambic)—possibly after *alembic*, meaning a still, or more likely after the village of Lembeek in Pajottenland. For the disappointed brewer, the only thing to do was dump it. But at some point, with so much spoiled beer on hand, one brewer either decided to keep some casks of it or just forgot about them, and then after a year or so when he tapped one of them, he found the off flavour had mellowed into something...well, palatable, especially if you blended it with some fresh beer. And people actually acquired a taste for it. Some brewers went further, adding fruit and perhaps caramelized sugar at first to mask the odd flavour, but at some point they found they had created a new style of beer. It was called *gueuze* and was often named after the fruit—*kriek* (wild cherry), *framboise* (raspberry) or *cassis* (blackcurrant)—that had been macerated and added. These styles have persisted to the present. And because they are never less than a year old and commonly two, with high alcohol content from a long secondary fermentation in corked, wired, champagne-style bottles, they are treated like champagne with foil capsules and decorated tissue paper. Maybe you can't make a silk purse out of a sour beer, but with patience you can make a wonderful, unique beer style that sells for a premium price.

When I worked for O'Keefe, the pitching yeast (yeast from a previous brew that has been cleaned up and is "pitched" into the wort to ferment it) was never exposed to the atmosphere. It was run from a totally enclosed fermenter through a sterile hose into a sterilized "yeast buggy" (a small tank on wheels with an airtight lid), mixed with cold, sterile water and put into a small refrigerated room for storage. The yeast room, which had a tiled floor and walls that were regularly washed down and sprayed with sanitizer, was used for no other purpose and had positive air pressure supplied by sterile air. The wort delivery line from the brewhouse to the fermenters went through this room, and it was provided with fittings for injecting the yeast and aerating the wort with sterile air. Nobody was allowed into this room except the fermenter man and me, and then only for taking laboratory samples. Every batch of yeast and every fermentation was "plated out" in Petri dishes with nutrient medium and incubated to reveal the presence of beer spoilage organisms.

We would commonly get through a hundred generations of yeast before replacing it, and even then not because of contaminants but because it was "flagging" or sluggish in fermentation. If there is sufficient aeration, sluggish fermentations usually indicate some physiological problem with the yeast, perhaps from being stored too long between brews. Yeast likes to be active, and a vigorous fermentation is your best way to ward off infections, even if you have some contaminating bugs in there.

No small craft brewery has such tight yeast-handling methods as I have described above, so some aerial contamination of the yeast is to be expected. I have trained some brewers in the lab techniques for detecting spoilage organisms, but craft brewers are busy people who often don't have the time for lab work, can't wait for the results of a five-day incubation and need to do something fast if there is a problem. The usual answer is to get some yeast from another brewery (but what secrets does *their* yeast contain?) or better yet order a litre or two of pure culture yeast from the catalogue of a specialist laboratory like Wyeast or White Labs. This will guarantee not only a culture free of contaminants but also a yeast specific to your style of beer.

Regularly replacing yeast with pure cultures is like setting the ship back on course, but it is an expense, and besides, pure cultures may be slow to get going and may at first produce beers with atypical flavours not quite the same as those made when the yeast hits its stride and is used to the characteristics of your particular wort. For this reason, brewers want to keep a good strain of yeast going for as long as possible. The following are some treatments that will help reduce microbial contaminants.

Yeast washing

A technique that has been used for centuries is simply to make a thin slurry of the newly cropped yeast by stirring clean cold water into it, leaving it in a cold room overnight, then decanting the supernatant liquid from the top. Repeat the procedure if you have the time. What have you done here? Well, a yeast cell has many times the mass of a 1 micron bacillus and will sink to the bottom of your container while the tiny contaminants remain in suspension. Pour off the supernatant, and you have also dumped a large number of your enemies. Simple! This should be done on every batch of yeast collected for further pitching. But make sure your dilution water is sterile or close to it.

Acid washing

Bacteria are much more susceptible to low pH values (the measure of acidity/alkalinity) than yeast is. (If you don't know about pH and you want to be a brewmaster, it's about time you learned!) By lowering the pH of your yeast slurry to 2.8 and leaving it in the cold room for a couple of hours, most bacteria will be killed. You lower the pH by adding a stock solution of 20 percent tartaric or phosphoric acid, stirring it in while checking the pH with a hand-held pH meter.

Acid/persulfate washing

A more rigorous treatment is to do the acid wash, then add ammonium persulfate in an amount equal to 0.75 percent of the weight of the pitching yeast, stirring well for an hour before you wish to use it. Acid washing kills some yeast cells too, so be careful your contact times are not too long, and compensate for yeast kill-off by increasing the amount of yeast pitched by about a quarter from that normally used. The chemicals in the washes are metabolized in the fermentation.

Microbial fault detection

Aside from plating every sample in Petri dish cultures and waiting for the incubated results, there are some things you can do to pick up incipient infections that depend on olfaction, a fancy name for taste and smell. The taste buds on the tongue are quite coarse in what they can detect, but the dime-size olfaction receptor in the back of the nose is as sensitive as a gas chromatograph worth thousands of dollars. In college I was astounded when told that the nose is capable of discerning ten thousand different odours, but recently researchers using more sophisticated methods have shown this to be an underestimation of at least ten times. Not only that, but they showed it is not a case of being born with it or not. People can be trained to have such sensitivity. How do you train your palate (or nose) to this level? Well, obviously you don't smoke and don't eat or drink flavourful foods for at least an hour before tasting samples. You clean your palate with water and assess your samples in a clean room with no competing odours in the air. All samples should be at room temperature so the aromatics are released readily. You smell and smell again before tasting while agitating the sample by swirling. You don't talk to your fellow tasters, and you write down your impressions.

Whenever you have a problem, don't just throw the beer out. Identify the cause and keep some of it in a capped, labelled bottle for future reference. In this way you can develop a sensitivity to all the common defects of beer by setting up a "reference library" of bottles of beer or water containing all of the common problems, such as lactic (lactobacillus); acetic (airborne contamination); phenolic (wild yeast); diacetyl and acetaldehyde (fermentation problems); wet cardboard (oxidized, old); dimethyl and hydrogen sulphides (stuck fermentations, insufficient "gassing off" of CO_2 from closed fermenters); skunky or mercaptan (sunstruck).

Forcing test

A simple way to "force" a problem to appear in finished beer or unpitched wort is to incubate capped bottles at 37°C for three or four days and then check the odour and taste of the sample. Any spoilage organisms will have their growth speeded up, as will biochemical reactions, so you should pick it up as a flavour/odour defect. (Don't have an incubator? You can make one in a cupboard with a small light bulb, wired through a thermostat. It's accurate enough for this kind of work, and it costs peanuts.)

Stuck fermentations

Transferring the wort into the fermenter is the best time to inject the pitching yeast and bubble in some oxygen (or sterile air) to give the yeast that necessary "kick" to boost its initial growth. Remember that, although alcoholic fermentation is an anaerobic process, *Saccharomyces* requires oxygen for its own reproduction, and a lack of it will result in sluggish growth and "stuck" fermentations. Simple in-line stainless fittings that fasten to the fermenter inlet/outlet valve are the best way to inject yeast slurry and oxygen into the wort without exposing it to the atmosphere. Twenty-litre soda-pop-type cans that are of sanitary construction and are pressure-rated work well as yeast containers. The yeast slurry is forced into the wort stream with top pressure from a CO_2 bottle. Oxygenators have a sintered stainless "thimble" like a fish tank aerator welded inside the wort line fitting with a small stainless line plus ball valve. When connected to an oxygen tank by flex hose, this thimble will release a fine cloud of oxygen that aerates the wort stream. Sometimes oxygenators may be fitted inside the tanks to "rouse" stuck fermentations.

How the brewer deals with a stuck fermentation may illustrate the difference between a brewer with practical experience and one with laboratory skills. The brewer will know that he should "rouse" the brew and oxygenate it, and if that works—well, everything is okay. But if the brew doesn't respond, what then? I would be examining a suspension of the yeast under the microscope at 450x to see if there were any anomalies compared with the normal appearance of the yeast, indicating some physiological change. You can also stain the suspension with methylene blue, which stains dead cells blue, and make an estimation of the number of dead cells versus live ones in a population of pitching yeast. Healthy yeast should be 98 percent or more live cells and not show any abnormality of shape. Of course, this implies that you have a microscope, know how to use it and have examined enough yeast to know what normal looks like.

Conditioning

The brewer will be monitoring his fermentation as constantly and closely as a mother does her baby, checking its temperature, its growth (by hydrometer readings, which should show a progressive decrease in specific gravity as the sugars in the wort are turned into alcohol and CO_2), its smell and taste. A typical wort with an original gravity of, say, 1040 SG, pitched at 20°C (68°F), will show a drop of only a few degrees in the first 24 hours as the yeast increases its numbers exponentially (lag phase). However, the next 48 hours should see a vigorous fermentation with the specific gravity dropping rapidly to about 1020, followed by a steady decrease to 1010 five or six days into the fermentation. Cooling is gradually applied at this stage, and the fermenter is bunged to restrict the escape of CO_2 from the vent in order to make it dissolve in the beer and achieve carbonation. Depending on how sweet or dry you want the finished product, and how much unfermentable sugars and soluble protein are in your wort, it should bottom out around 1005 to 1003 SG. (Incidentally, alcohol-by-volume is calculated by subtracting the end gravity of the beer from the original gravity and multiplying this figure by .102.) At this point the brewer transfers the beer to a conditioning tank in a cold room, where it is stored at temperatures cold enough to promote settling of the remaining yeast cells and other sediment—mainly protein, which is precipitated out of solution through the chilling process. Alternatively, if he is using cylindro-conical unitanks, which ferment and condition in a single tank, he applies more cooling to lower the temperature to about 4°C. The deposited "spent yeast" can be removed daily from the outlet valve on the lower cone of the unitank. In fermenters with a shallow bottom, I use a short (4- to 6-inch) riser or upstand pipe that fits into the outlet and retains most of the yeast while the "green" (young) beer is decanted off. Big breweries rely on filtration to remove sediment, but many craft brewers prefer the gentler treatment of adding finings, an isinglass colloid, which collects sediment particles as it slowly drops to the bottom of the tank. Others add a "final polish" filtration to the packaged beer. However, avoiding filtration altogether leaves a beer with a fuller body, better head and better flavour, though aging times may be longer.

But there is more happening in conditioning than mere settling and sediment removal as any brewer will attest, tasting green beer right from the fermenter and the same beer three or four weeks later when it has undergone flavour maturation. The yeasty taste and sulphitic smell have disappeared, allowing the pleasant aromatics to come forth. The intense bitterness of hopped wort has mellowed into a nice combination with the malt flavours; this is what we call "well balanced." And if you look at a graph of the chromatography analysis of green beer, it looks like a cardiac scan gone wild. The trace shows a rugged terrain of jagged peaks and valleys denoting giant molecules of protein and complex chemicals, by-products of fermentation, and long-chain alcohols (fusel oils), diacetyl and sulphur compounds. If you compare this with a graph of the aged product, you will see the rough peaks have been reduced and rounded off, and some have disappeared entirely, replaced by smoother traces of much smaller molecular weight aromatic compounds. The rough edges of the flavour have literally been rounded off. This is why it is not a good practice to rush the product through by early filtration. Yeast cells present in conditioning will actually reabsorb undesirable compounds like fusel oils and diacetyl as the beer ages.

Keeping air away from the beer throughout its aging and preparation for serving, bottling or kegging is a major concern, since air not only contains spoilage organisms but also produces undesirable oxidation products. It used to be common practice to add antioxidants like potassium metabisulphite to beer (this is still widely practised with wine) to combat air pickup and bacterial growth. But in modern plants with closed fermenters and tight storage tanks that are (or should be) purged with CO_2 before filling, there is only a very small chance of air being introduced. The main dangers are when the beer is transferred from tank to tank during filtration and packaging. Beer should always be treated as gently as possible after fermentation, which is all the more reason for the craft brewer to minimize transfers and do away with filtration if possible. The ideal set-up is the brewpub where the beer after fermentation is transferred once, with finings added, to a tank for, say, two to three weeks (for ales) of conditioning, then decanted to a serving tank to fine and settle for four to seven days before serving direct to the bar without the hassle and possible air pickup during filtration, kegging or bottling. Increasing the aging time always improves the product up to about two months. It's hard to beat for preserving the natural flavour and body of the beer with minimal labour and risk of contamination or oxidation.

But in a microbrewery where the product is always packaged, production is preeminent, and shelf life and clarity are prime considerations, filtration becomes a necessary evil. Or does it? Sean Hoyne, whom I trained at Swans to believe that the best beers are unfiltered, has carried on that credo with his Hoyne Brewing plant in Victoria, where he produces large quantities of keg and bottled beer of high quality without filtering. He uses unitanks, uses cold temperature fining for conditioning, transfers to bright beer tanks, and allows plenty of time. And his business is growing so fast that, in his words, "I've got a tiger by the tail." I hope that Sean can keep his integrity and his quality as the demand for his products increases, because so often success and the pressure to increase production lead to shorter aging times, filtration or other compromises.

Filtering to achieve absolute clarity and lengthy shelf life is a tricky, multi-stage process. The beer must be chilled to as low a temperature as possible for 24 hours to promote precipitation of proteins that might otherwise appear as chill haze when the beer is packaged. Low temperatures will also help the settling of the remaining yeast cells. The beer is then run through a filter using cellulose pads and/ or diatomaceous earth (D.E.) as the filtering agent. D.E., which is the remains of ancient diatoms, comes in the form of a fine white powder and under the microscope looks a bit like crushed seashells. Since it is pure silica, it does not dissolve in, react to or alter the flavour of beer. (It is also widely used in clarifying wine.) Fine stainless-steel filter screens designed to trap the particles of sediment are coated with D.E. by making a slurry of it in beer, then recirculating it through the filter until the liquid coats the plates and runs clear (precoating). The main run through the filter then begins, with more D.E. slurry injected into the beer flow with a dosing pump (body feed). This continuous addition to the coating on the filter screens keeps sediment from blocking the filter. The filters are provided with pressure gauges on the inlet and outlet, and the difference will indicate if the filter is getting blocked, as the inlet pressure will rise and the outlet pressure will drop. Any abrupt changes in the pressures will cause the D.E. to break away from the screens and spoil the run. This is made worse if the CO_2 level of the beer is high, as any drop in the pressure inside the filter will cause bubbles to form and break up the D.E. coating. For this reason, major breweries filter their beer at low carbonation levels. They collect the CO_2

from fermentation, clean it, compress and chill it until it becomes liquid, then store it for recarbonating the "bright beer" after filtration. But the cost of such a CO_2 treatment plant is way beyond anything a small brewery could afford.

You can see why I call filtration "tricky" and why it is a good idea for craft brewers to avoid it altogether. In any case, even D.E. filtration is not the complete answer if you are looking for long-term biological stability at room temperatures. Since beer spoilage organisms are in the range of 1 micron (a thousandth of a millimetre) in size, even the finest grade of D.E. will not completely remove them, though the beer may be acceptably clear in appearance. Big breweries may follow D.E. filtration by passing the beer through a "final polish filter" that uses cellulose pads and even a third pass through membrane filters of 0.5 micron pore size (ultrafiltration) to remove bacteria. A recent TV ad by a big American brewery boasts of its "triple-filtered" beer, but as an older brewmaster once said to me, "What is left after you've filtered the guts out of it?" Excessive filtration can remove the soluble proteins and carbohydrates that give the beer body and produce a good head on a glass of beer.

So, given enough time, settling and the use of isinglass finings will give your beer acceptable clarity, and so will a D.E. filter if you have less time and fewer tanks, but you may run into microbial problems if your bottles stand for months on a shelf at room temperature. Keeping the product cold is the answer. However, in the old days the only outlets for bottled product in BC were the government liquor stores, which had no coolers, and some small breweries ran into problems with biological off-flavours and beer being returned, which resulted in delisting by the liquor board. Some of these breweries had to tighten up their practices as far as sanitizing and preventing air pick-up, which was not a bad thing. But a welcome development was the licensing of cold beer and wine stores, where all beer was kept in coolers. The popularity of these outlets has forced the government stores to install coolers as well. Slowly, slowly, craft beer has fought off its problems, and the outlets are realizing it is worthwhile catering to it.

Over the past thirty years, people have developed a taste for craft beers, getting used to the fact that they are not the same—*are not supposed to be the same*—as the mainstream lagers. They are unique, and each craft beer is different from all other craft beers. The name itself encompasses two dozen or more beer styles and a whole range of flavours, colours, potency and hoppiness. They are a challenge to the palate, not just something to quench your thirst or "get a buzz on." People have come to realize that some bottle-conditioned beers or hefeweizens *are not meant to be clear*, that yeast is part of the picture, part of the flavour spectrum. And I am reminded of a hilarious cartoon from CAMRA that I saw in a newspaper in the UK: two tweedy, bearded guys are headed into a pub that boasts a sign announcing: "REAL ALE—with bits floating in it!"

For a long time the beer marketplace in North America was dominated by beer as a streamlined commodity, mass-produced in consolidated super-efficient factories where the cheapest methods of production were tied to the bottom line, and the beer companies' biggest expenditure was on marketing and advertising as they tried to convince consumers of a basic lie—that their beer was the best. Meanwhile, Europeans had been enjoying a rainbow variety of beers for centuries, just as they had with wines.

It is high time that we on this continent had the same opportunities. It is time that honest, barley-malted, hoppy, flavourful beers reasserted their rightful position in the minds and mouths of drinkers. This is the responsibility and the reward of a brewmaster in a craft brewery.

15) Where to From Here?

THREE DECADES ON FROM THE DAY JOHN MITCHELL AND I opened the Horseshoe Bay Brewery with its tiny brewing plant and only our joint enthusiasm and a lot of hope that enough people would like our beer to justify the investment and our work, the craft beer scene is unrecognizable. Not only in Vancouver and BC but right across Canada and the US, craft beer sales have exploded beyond anything I would have thought possible. A tsunami of new beer styles—or old beer styles revived—has swept the continent. Now it is difficult to go into any pub, tavern, bar or licensed restaurant and not find good-quality craft beer available. And I smile to think of the smug quote from a big brewery executive who was asked by a reporter for his comment on the opening of the Horseshoe Bay Brewery: "If it was a good idea, we would have done it by now."

The situation has been turned on its head from before the 1980s, when the choice went by many names—light lager, bland lager, and pale adjunct lager—with a little sprinkling of imports hinting that, yes, there might be something else out there. The Big Three brewers had gobbled up the many small local breweries with the distinctive products that had existed prior to World War II, consolidating not only their brand names but also corrupting the nature and character of their beers to a uniform, bland entity made with large helpings of cornstarch, corn syrup or rice adjunct to replace portions of the barley malt. Why was this done? Not to improve the product, as was claimed, but to make it cheaper to produce. The money that they saved went into massive marketing campaigns designed to persuade us that this new light beer was the beer of the post-war generation—the young, active, with-it crowd of both men and women. The old beer was for the old guys, hanging out in smoky bars, pubs and saloons. It had a bad image—too heavy, too dark, too hoppy.

There is an inescapable analogy with the replacement of nutritious, whole-wheat bread with bland white Wonder Bread that keeps forever with the aid of preservatives. Beer and bread have been the mainstays of the human diet for millennia, but the plethora of foods that became available in the developed world reduced them to an incidental role. Beer became an accessory to leisure, fun times, courting. Women didn't want that heavy, fattening, old-style beer, the marketing moguls told the breweries; they wanted something like wine, white wine. The brewers obliged.

But a decade or two before the craft beer revolution, an unsung revolt began happening in our kitchens. Housewives and mothers began rejecting the empty, flavourless white bread from the mega bakeries and baking their own from whole-wheat flour. They knew what was good for their families. It took a while for the bakery chains to catch on, but if you look on supermarket shelves today, you will find the bland, white, keep-forever breads marginalized. The big sellers are made fresh from whole wheat and a variety of grains right in the store or certainly locally. Thankfully, the same thing is happening with beer. The big brewers painted themselves into a corner, seduced by their own marketing hype. A backlash was inevitable. I was just one of the first to write an article that became a revolutionary pamphlet because it said something that many had thought—that good beer, flavourful and nutritious beer, had become debased. It had lost out to a mass-produced, pale imitation of itself. The reaction was an idea whose time had come.

Craft beer across Canada has gone from zero percent of the market in 1982 to over 6 percent today and growing. In BC it is said to be 10 percent, and in hotbeds like Victoria and Portland, it's probably twice that. Craft beer in the US occupied 7.8 percent of the market in 2013, and the slogan for real beer buffs became "Twenty percent by 2020." Here is what Gary Fish, owner of Deschutes Brewery in Oregon—now the third largest craft brewery in the US—told the US Brewers Association when he was its chair in 2014:

> The "twenty-by-twenty" objective for our craft community is an aspirational goal with an inspiring symmetry. I am convinced it is within our reach if we, as an industry, continue to focus on our strengths and passions—making and delivering high-quality, innovative, full-flavoured beer to craft beer enthusiasts.

There were close to ninety craft breweries in BC in 2015, and the number is still rising. Perhaps the most encouraging thing is that this growth is happening despite the overall beer market being flat and with the big boys selling cheaper beer. In addition, with a few exceptions, craft beer breweries are almost 100 percent independently owned.

Can this phenomenal growth continue? Probably not—certainly not at this pace. As in nature, there are checks and balances to the growth of any organism that finds a favourable ecological niche (a market, in business parlance) and exploits it with exponential growth. Location, space to expand, nutrition (cash flow), innovation to counter competition, continued health and vitality are all as necessary to a company as to a living creature. Already there have been bright, new craft breweries that have closed their doors or been taken over because they lacked one or more of these essentials.

Today, if I were a starry-eyed young brewer who had learned how to brew good beer in small batches and figured I could please and amaze the public with my products and make a living at it, and if I had raised $70,000 or so for start-up as John Mitchell did in Horseshoe Bay in 1982, I would think twice about it and probably keep my money in my pocket. We had *no* competition when we launched Bay Ale. We were *it*, and the only place you could get a pint of our beer was in the Troller Pub. It was an enviable situation, and not one you are likely to find today except in a few small, remote communities that have yet to discover craft beer. But the problem with such locales is that there aren't enough drinkers to keep the beer (and the cash) flowing. Beer is a relatively low-cost item that requires volume to pay for your ingredients, your overhead, your rent, excise taxes and wages—never mind marketing—and produce a profit. Volume means being where the people are, and today that is where you'll find your competitors. And today's competitors have operations that do not have a mere seventy grand in equipment; they are more likely to have a half-million or more invested. "Small breweries" have become considerably larger and more professional and business-like.

If you want to read about the reality of starting a small brewery on a shoestring, get a copy of *So You Want to Start a Brewery?* by Tony Magee, who started Lagunitas Brewing Company in northern California with $30,000, a collection of used and discounted equipment, and himself as the sole employee. Reading his account of his battles with banks, his travails with the taxman, hocking his house, his deals with distributors and showdowns with shareholders, you will think, Yikes! Who would ever get into this business? But Tony believed in his beers and he was excited by the challenge, and today Lagunitas is one of the larger craft beer producers in California.

Even some well-established brands have found themselves in trouble. After eighteen years in business and just as many Canadian Brewing Awards to its credit, R&B Brewing in Vancouver faced bankruptcy early in 2015 and had to lay off staff, leaving owners Barry Benson and Rick Dellow to keep the operation going while they tried to find new investment. Meanwhile, the craft brewing scene was shocked: How could this happen to such an established operation? "It's been a couple of years in the making," said Rick in an interview. "We lost sales but maintained the same staffing." (They had nine, which is a lot for a draft-only operation.) "We've always been on the edge of making a profit one year and a small loss the next...then having two or three years of losses, we got to the point where we couldn't sustain it."

And take note: when R&B started in 1997 in the old Brewery Creek area near Main Street in East Vancouver, it was the only brewery around. Today there are no fewer than six in the vicinity, and the area is now drolly referred to as "Yeast Vancouver." When the BC government relaxed the rules a few years ago and allowed microbreweries to have 50-seat "tasting rooms," many leapt at the option. R&B did not. It didn't have the space or the cash. However, according to Iain Hill, now of Strange Fellows Brewing, "Our tasting room is the difference between making it and not." And a footnote on R&B: in March 2015 it was announced that Howe Sound Brewing would be taking over the brewery, with each company's brands being made in both Vancouver and Squamish. This is a smart move for both because it means that Howe Sound will not need trucks shuttling up and down the Sea to Sky Highway to service Vancouver, and the R&B brand will still exist.

Matt Phillips, founder of the robust and growing Phillips Brewing Company in Victoria (which recently added its own malting plant), had this to say in an interview:

> A lot of people got into breweries because they saw it as a really easy way to make a buck. [They said] "It's a hot industry and it's growing and you can't lose money." The second you start to hear people say that, it's doomed. [Phillips Brewing is] getting to a point now where shelf space is so limited…that's one of the driving constraints on our industry right now. There's only so many taps, there's only so much shelf space. There's a lot of appetite to try new and different beers, but even that isn't infinite, to be honest.

Ken Beattie, executive director of the fifty-six-member BC Craft Brewers Guild, adds this:

> People get into it for the passion and the love of
> beer. And then they're stuck into the business.
> They need a sales team, distribution...growth
> seems to incrementally leap. And if you don't
> have a solid business plan...you're going to get
> left behind.

In the beginning the big boys were the only competition for craft brewers, so they developed into a happy alliance that cooperated against a common threat. This fellowship is mostly still intact in Canada, though cracks have begun to emerge in recent years across the border. For many years now the Boston Beer Company has been the largest craft brewery there, selling 2,125,000 barrels in 2012, far ahead of Sierra Nevada at 966,000 and Deschutes at 255,000. Boston is the creation of Jim Koch, a smart Harvard MBA graduate who saw an opportunity in the early success of the real beer movement and decided to exploit it. He was armed with little more than a recipe from his great-grandfather, a lot of business savvy and the ability to push the envelope when it came to promotion.

But the business-suited Koch is about as far from the gumboots-and-coveralls founders of most small breweries as you can get, and he is detested by many of them. Why? In 1983 when Koch decided to get into the business, he did what few starry-eyed, beer-loving young brewers do: he studied the market and the cost of building a brewery and making beer. He found that the $300,000 he could raise would fall far short of what a serious brewery would cost, never mind wages, advertising and promotion. Then he realized that there were a few older breweries in the north-eastern US whose businesses were faltering, and they had empty tanks and excess capacity. Why not have them brew his beer under contract? And the era of contract brews began. Koch got Stroh's Brewery in Pennsylvania to brew his beer, and it came on the market without him spending a penny on building, plant or equipment while saving his capital for radio and TV promotion. It didn't faze him that his Boston Lager was not being made in Boston, and he had the bright idea of draping his bottles in the flag and calling his mythical brewery Samuel Adams, after one of America's founding fathers. "Samuel Adams, brewer, pa-triot" reads his tag line. Except Adams was never a brew-er. He was a maltster, and when he failed at that, he went into politics.

In 1985 I attended the Great American Beer Festival (GABF) in Denver, a three-day event featuring craft brews and culminating in a day of public tasting of hundreds of beers from the booths of scores of craft brewers. With your entrance ticket, you were given a ballot and asked to name the best beers in the show—first, second and third. That was the year Samuel Adams Boston Lager made its debut. It was easy to spot the company's booth because it had a bright Stars and Stripes motif with pretty young women serving the beer. Koch was not in evidence. The other brewers' booths looked dull by comparison, usually manned by the brewers themselves and displaying a few cases and kegs of beer. Meanwhile, word had got around about the true origins of "Boston Lager," and the real brew-ers at the festival were not happy to see the people with Sam Adams hats and T-shirts in the crowd. When the votes were tabulated at the end of the day, the winner of Best Beer in America, as the sponsors modestly called their award, was Samuel Adams's Boston Lager. The announcement was greeted with a wave of boos from the booths. I had sampled the Sam Adams product, and though it was a quality, all-malt lager, it was far from being the best beer in the show, especially against products covering the spectrum from *weissbiers* to Imperial Russian stouts. This did not bother Koch. His beer cases and advertising immediately began boasting "Best Beer in America" and his sales took off. His Boston Lager won again in 1986 and 1987, and the boos grew louder from the crowd of 4,500 in attendance. The real brewers were incensed because they said Koch was buying votes with freebies and free tickets to the convention. Confronted, Koch admitted that his salesmen gave free tickets to his beer distributors and customers "as an incentive to attend the festival." Some brewers announced they would cease to attend the GABF, and the organizers, the Association of Brewers, faced a torrent of disapproval. The association was a group of Denver businessmen, not brewers, who had been appointed by festival organizers Charlie Papazian and Daniel Bradford, amateur brewers and writers who put out *The New Brewer* and *Zymurgy* magazines. Fearing the criticism would torpedo the GABF, Papazian and Bradford shifted the judging the following year from the public to blind tasting by a group of professional brewers and certified beer experts, who evaluated the merits of beers in thirty-six style categories. The judging itself was supervised by the national Beer Judge Certification Program. Giveaways were restricted to having a dollar in value, and the GABF earned back its credibility.

But by this time Koch was off and running, leading the craft pack in beer sales (a position he has never relinquished), a loner who would rather spend time hosting beer distributors than hanging out with other brewers, which is a lesson in marketing hype over substance. His booming sales soon caught the attention of Bill Hambrecht of Hambrecht and Quist, a venture capital company, who offered Koch $7 million for a 20 percent interest in the Boston Beer Company. From a $300,000 investment, Koch was now swimming in capital. To achieve some credibility as a "Boston brewery," he bought the little old Haffenreffer Brewery in a rundown part of the city, and for an additional expenditure of $200,000 installed a plant from the closure of a brewery in New York City. But this was mere appearances. As Koch expanded sales into most states in the union, he contracted with a number of breweries across the country. He enraged the craft brewers of Oregon by invading their bustling market, launching beers labelled "from the Oregon Ale and Beer Company," another company of his, although they were actually made in a contract deal with a brewery in Washington state. Gary Fish from Deschutes and the other Oregon microbreweries (plus Anheuser-Busch!) forced Koch to state on the labels where the beer was made, and in time he gave up on his Oregon Ale caper.

Fortunately, we haven't seen the likes of Jim Koch in Canada—yet. The closest is Alexander Keith's, whose national TV ads pretend its IPA is made from an ancient recipe of its figurehead, brewed in his centuries-old brewery in Halifax. In fact, the brewery has been lovingly restored by its owners, the Labatt/Budweiser/InBev consortium, but only as a Disneyland-style backdrop where tour groups can listen to paid actors in period costume posing as brewers, maltsters and barmaids. They will even sing you a Nova Scotia song! But Alexander Keith's beer? It is brewed in a Labatt plant across town and in the company's chain of mega plants across the country. As for the recipe, well, you just have to taste it to know it's the same pale, bland, adjunct lager the big boys have been foisting on us for decades. Read how the IPA was rated by contributors to the independent blog site Beer Advocate. Here are two that are typical of two dozen reviews: "Gives Nova Scotia beers a bad reputation," and "Shame on you, Alexander Keiths/Labatts. There was a time when this beer stood out from the rest of the mass-produced lagers in Canada. An IPA? Not a chance. Give this a wide pass." Who knew that good old Alex Keith used corn adjunct in his beer in the 1800s? Let's see the recipe! Whenever a national TV campaign is pushing a beer allegedly made by a craft brewery, you should smell a rat. None of them would be able to afford such promotion.

Not that the small outfits are immune to duplicity. In Vancouver we now have a brewery putting out beer with pictures on the label of a nineteenth-century brewery with the name "Stanley Park Brewery, est. 1897." In fact, the beer is made by Turning Point Brewery in an industrial area of Annacis Island and has no connection whatsoever with the park, which is owned by the City of Vancouver, nor with the original brewery of 1897. And the claim that its little wind turbine provides all the power to run its brewery is a laughable attempt to appear "green." Good for beer writer Joe Wiebe for pointing this out and leaving this brewery out of the craft beer section of his *Craft Beer Revolution* guide. (Perhaps it should go in a "crafty beer" category!)

Similarly, there is deceit in selling beers named after local brands that used to be made in well-known locales but have since been sold and are produced elsewhere by other companies. Whistler Brewing (not to be confused with Mark James's Brewhouse brewpub in Whistler) and Bowen Island Brewing are two examples. Both are now made in Kamloops by Bear Brewing, which itself was bought by Big Rock of Calgary in 2003 when that brewery expanded into BC. Later still, the two brands were sold to the North Am Group.

Takeovers and make-overs abound. Shaftebury was one of the early successes in the microbrewery scene of Vancouver and, far from faltering, was on an upswing in 1999, dominating the Vancouver draft beer market and building a brand-new brewery on River Road, when it was bought by Okanagan Spring Brewery of Vernon, BC craft brewing's largest company. Note that this was not really about buying a brewery, since OK Spring promptly dismantled the old Shaftebury plant in East Vancouver and never finished the new one. Instead, it was about buying the healthy draft market that Shaftebury had established. OK Spring continued to put out Shaftebury products as a low-priced craft beer line, but its credibility declined compared with the days when it was East Vancouver's friendly neighbourhood brewery, and OK Spring soon sold the brand to Tree Brewing of Kelowna. But let the buyer beware of being bought. In 1996 OK Spring was purchased by Sleeman Breweries of Ontario, who apparently had no qualms about using adjunct in their beers if it suited them, and then Sleeman, overextended, was sold to the Japanese giant Sapporo in 2006. Is it any wonder that Okanagan Spring beers seem somewhat different now than when the Toblers started the brewery as a family concern in 1985?

Granville Island Brewing (GIB) occupies a unique location and a unique place in Vancouver's brewing history, being among the first microbreweries to open back in 1984. The peninsula, which lies on False Creek in the heart of the city, is an old industrial area that was being reinvented at that time with a world-class covered market, boutiques, yacht mooring, art galleries, live lobster shops and bookstores. What else was needed? A craft brewery, of course! Mitch Taylor, one of the founding fathers of the Granville Island redevelopment project, rounded up partners and investment to create a gem of a brewery. Its Island Lager was the first domestic, all-malt, German-style lager the city had tasted in recent memory, and it was a hit from day one, the darling of the with-it set.

If anything, GIB's problems stemmed from its great success. Granville Island has but one narrow access road to serve all the businesses plus the locals and tourists who flock there. Gridlock is the norm. If you're smart, you don't even bother to drive down there; you park your car and walk in. This is okay for shoppers and tourists, but a brewery needs access—truckloads of materials in, finished product out. In addition, the brewery lacked room and capital for expansion, and its big seller was its lagers, which take six weeks or more to age, so they were running out of beer. Eventually, these problems were solved by selling the company to Potter Distilling, which owned Calona Wines and Ben Ginter's old outfit in Prince George, Pacific Western Brewing. The big-selling GIB brands were now made in Kelowna, with the smaller ones still made on Granville Island. Then in 2009 it was sold again, this time to Creemore Springs, which itself had been acquired by (gulp!) Molson Coors, and the big boys snuck into the craft beer market by the back door. GIB's most popular brands are now made in the giant Molson plant five minutes away from the Island, but the original brewery brews seasonal specialties and one-off experimental brews. Manager Joe Goetz, describing what Island Lager was like in the early days compared to what it is now, is quoted in *Beer Quest West* as saying, "It was initially fuller bodied and hoppier. We had to make it more conventional; it was too off-mainstream for many." Huh? Now it's been mainstreamed...

Perhaps the best way for a craft operation to stay independent and not get steamrolled by the competition, face bankruptcy and/or be bought out is to find a town or locale where you are the only brewery around, develop your own unique beer styles and brands, build a reputation with the locals, and don't grow so fast that you get overextended to the banks and become a choice morsel for the big guys. Small European breweries have been making atypical, non-mainstream products for centuries. These local beers often use unique malts and other ingredients. They are finicky, take too long to make, or have flavours that appeal to a smaller market, and they are therefore ignored by the mega breweries, which are only interested in products for the mass market. The Belgian lambics, Gueuze, Wits and Abbey beers are prime examples. Germany has many regional and seasonal specialties, including Kölsch in Cologne, Alt in Düsseldorf, Dortmunder in Dortmund, and Bock and Doppelbock in Einbeck and Munich. Marzenbier is a March specialty in Bavaria; Bamberg is noted for its smoky-flavoured Rauchbier. Bavaria boasts an amazing one thousand breweries, of which only a handful are owned by big conglomerates—a testament to the value accorded to local styles and brewing techniques that go back centuries. In many small towns the breweries were (and some still are) owned by the town itself and administered by the town council, so important was it to keep the beer bearing the town's name local, authentic, brewed by traditional methods and out of the hands of private owners who might be tempted to sell out. Britain, in contrast, which not long ago boasted a score of unique beer styles, has fallen victim to big-money buyouts, and though the new owners still offer the once-famous brands, it is in name only. Ironically, the best places in the UK to find authentic versions of the old milds, bitters, porters, IPAS, pale ales, barley wines, brown ales, sweet and dry stouts are the new wave of brewpubs and microbreweries. Remember this, those of you who wish to get into the business: in the minds and mouths of a discerning public it is quality, authenticity, uniqueness and honesty in ingredients, recipes, production, aging and presentation that will always win out over Big Brew hype and advertising. Ask yourself where you'd rather go out to eat—McDonald's or the small, local, ethnic restaurant that always has a lineup out the door? Of course, you say, I'd like to go to the ethnic restaurant but McDonald's is cheaper. Sure it is. It's bound to be, just as Labatt/Budweiser and Molson Coors are cheaper because of mass production and cheap, adjunct-laden ingredients. But people will pay for quality, the evidence being the growth of the craft beer market *despite* the beer business as a whole showing no growth.

People appreciate novelty. They like to try something new, and if they like it, they will come back to it again and again. Most small breweries are having some success copying known European beer styles. A few are venturing into the land of originality, and while not many have profited from it, there are those who have. In Chapter 10, I talked about the amazing success of Gary Fish with Deschutes Brewery and his daring decision to feature Black Butte Porter as the flagship brand. Today, Black Butte Porter is the second-biggest selling porter in the US. As a brewer, you have to believe. And you have to follow through with continued quality.

Sam Calagione started Dogfish Head Brewery in Delaware with a tiny 10-gallon brewing plant in his brewpub (it cost him $20,000) and a belief in producing "off-centered ales for off-centered people." He did everything himself—brewing, making dogfish tap handles, driving the delivery truck, designing menus, performing publicity stunts—everything. In the first year, he experimented with thirty different styles of beer! With something of a carefree attitude, he tried adding apricots, grapes, raisins, maple syrup, spices and spruce needles, but he noted every change on his brew sheets as well as the reaction from his "R&D Department"—the brewpub bar crowd. Not all of his experiments were successful, but slowly word got out about the little brewery in Delaware and its unique brews. While his wife, Mariah, used social media to get the message out, listing new beers and soliciting opinions on them, Sam began hosting a show called *Brew Masters* on the Discovery Channel, which gave him more exposure. With the brewpub a financial success, in 1997 Sam made the decision to build a 50 BBL production brewery in nearby Milton. Building this taught him important lessons, among them that with a brewpub you have other streams of income than just beer sales—such as food, wine and mixed drinks—and direct daily contact with your customers. A brewery just has beer, and its market is the anonymous masses out there. In trying to sell that beer, you are dealing with distributors and liquor store owners, not your public. These things, plus the soaring building and equipment costs, put his brewery in a deficit position for years, and this deficit had to be made up with the brewpub profits. Dogfish Head walked the high wire of solvency for a long time before Sam's determination and increased public acceptance of his products set it back on the road to profitability. Since then, he has developed a keen sense of business, management, and the worth of employees while retaining his maverick off-centred approach to his beers. His book *Brewing Up a Business* is an entertaining must-read for anyone thinking of becoming a craft brewer.

Closer to home a few brewers are carving out niches for their products by going down the road less travelled. Crannóg Ales is a small brewery on a 10-acre certified organic farm in Sorrento, in the Shuswap area of BC. Brian MacIsaac and Rebecca Kneen thought a brewery would be a great addition to their farm, but it would also have to be fully organic and completely integrated into the farm operation. The result is Canada's first certified organic farmhouse brewery. They grow their own organic hops from rootstock obtained from New Zealand and use malt from organic barley growers in Alberta, now available through Gambrinus Malting in nearby Armstrong. (Organic malt is catching on with many small brewers, such as Nelson Brewing Company, which recently went all-organic.) MacIsaac and Kneen are also into recycling: the Crannóg brewery uses the old Horseshoe Bay equipment with which John Mitchell and I started the whole craft brewing thing in 1982! Spent grains from the brewery are fed to the pigs, which in turn provide fertilizer for the hops. The hop yards have proved so successful that Crannóg is now able to offer organic rootstock to others, and Kneen has produced a book on small-scale hop production to help people get started. Their line of Irish-style ales includes their wonderful Back Hand of God Stout, which is the best domestically produced stout I have tasted.

I love these mom-and-pop operations, which now include Townsite Brewing in Powell River, Mount Begbie in Revelstoke, Arrowhead in Invermere, Salt Spring Island Ales, and Hoyne Brewing in Victoria. Sean Hoyne, who started with a leased 10 BBL plant in 1991, replaced it with a 30 BBL plant just three years later, and now employs wife Chantal as business manager and son Dylan, along with a half-dozen others, on the brew crew. Small operations are welcomed by the small towns in which most are located, adding to the local identity and giving people something to boast about. Chloe Smith and Cédric Dauchot (BC's only accredited Belgian brewmaster) added more than a brewery and a line of special and Belgian-style beers to Powell River: they started a family there! The youth of the craft beer owner/operators is one of the movement's strong vital signs, with many still in their thirties.

The public perception of what good beer is all about has changed as the brewing business returned to its roots, to local operations in small towns—of which Canada has thousands. Before the advent of long-distance freight transportation and refrigeration, it was only natural that beer, which is 95 percent water, was made and sold close to a good source of water and grain. Shipping long distances was out of the question. Now with the reappearance of alternatives, people have realized that what the big boys have been selling them is marketing hype, not substance, not good, wholesome, satisfying beer. You can put as many fancy names and advertising come-ons to it as you like, but bland, adjunct lager is still bland, adjunct lager.

The drinking public is getting smarter: people are not drinking more, but they are drinking (and paying for) quality. Witness the growth of craft beers while sales of mainstream products remain static. The variety of beers available now is astonishing. My doctor recently commented to me, "It's amazing the boom in the craft beer types available in the last ten years. [It used to be that] if you were invited out to dinner, you asked what type of wine would be appropriate. Now you think about what style of craft beer they might like." Craft beer is no longer just an interesting alternative to mainstream lager. Like wine, it has established itself as a separate, multi-faceted category, worthy of respect by the consumer. This is a huge shift.

I don't see any return to the bad old days of the big boys controlling the beer market, though they will still sell vast amounts of beer, simply because what they offer is cheaper, available everywhere, and hugely promoted. According to a *Guardian Weekly* article from November 2015, "One company will supply nearly a third of the world's beer from next year, after...Anheuser-Busch InBev reached a final agreement for its £71bn takeover of Britain's SABMiller. The Budweiser owner AB InBev employs 155,000 people, compared with 70,000 at SAB Miller. Their combined revenues total $73bn, which is higher than companies such as Google or PepsiCo." So what? That still leaves two-thirds of the world's beer market, which is a hell of an ocean for craft breweries to swim in. In a way the *Guardian* report indicates a kind of desperation by the mass beer moguls. They have given up trying to push feeble "innovative" products such as ice beer, low-cal beer, flavoured beer, premium beers and draft beer in bottles and have once again taken up that good old boardroom game of improving profit for the shareholders by reducing costs via buyouts, consolidation of production plants, adding more adjunct, speeding up production and uniformity of brands.

Why don't the biggies get into making craft beer? It's an intriguing question, but the simple answer is they can't. They can't make beer in small batches because it's not cost-effective. They don't have equipment that's small enough, and even if they did, it would take a separate staff to run it. Using whole malted grains instead of cutting the grist with adjunct would also add to the cost. As for unfiltered beer and using distinctive bottles as most craft breweries do, when you look at the small potential market, it's not worth the trouble. Mass-production breweries need a mass market, and the mass market in North America drinks bland light lager. Since that is what they know how to do, that is what they promote, and that is what brings in the bucks. Try and tell an executive of Coors or Budweiser that the future lies in bold, hoppy real ales when they are selling and making millions from a zillion gallons of adjunct lager. But that's okay. Craft brewers are not aiming for the mass market. We're aiming for the people who know how to savour malty, hoppy beers that fill them up with real flavour and nutrition. A brewmaster in a small brewery might have an inspiration: "Let's make a triple-hopped Irish stout and see how it sells." And he goes ahead and does it. The brewmaster (more accurately called a production manager now) in a mega brewery could never make a decision like that. A weighty issue like launching a new product would be made in the boardroom with hefty input from the marketing department, which would demand a hundred thousand dollars for promotion plus the say on label and carton design, advertising, marketing and even, yes, what goes into the product. It must not be too dark, too heavy, too highly hopped—in fact, not too different from the mass-market brands already out there. "Don't worry," say the marketing execs. "The difference is all in the marketing." They would look with distaste on a hefty stout because their sales research tells them exactly how small the market would be, and the mere idea would be laughed out of existence.

What is driving the craft beer revolution is the belief that we're on to something here—innovation and integrity, brewers and consumers both believing in the product, in authenticity, in healthy stuff locally brewed by folk you may know, and drinking to enjoy it with friends instead of getting whacked. We have created a market of drinkers who relish new products—beers with character—made locally, beers to talk about with friends. Why do you need advertising when you have a high-quality, unique product whose excellence is spread by word of mouth? Let the product speak for itself.

I have been given a lifetime achievement award by CAMRA, and brewers have named beers after me, and in turn I would like to raise a glass to them. Here's to the brewers! If I was the spark that ignited a love of good beer in them, they are the ones who carried the torch forward. They are the ones at the crest of the craft beer tsunami. The beer scene will never be the same again.

Cheers!

Acknowledgements

A BIG THANK YOU FOR THE HELP OF THE FOLLOWING:
Edgewood Community Internet Society; the team at Harbour Publishing—Howard White, Betty Keller, Daniela Hajdukovic, Nicola Goshulak and Peter Robson; brewers Sean Hoyne, Andrew Tessier and Gary Fish; my niece, Lin Clifton; Joe Wiebe; and George Law.

Recommended Reading List

Textbooks

Association of the Society of Brewing Chemists. *Methods of Analysis*, 1978. Essential for all your laboratory work. Covers both chemistry and microbiology.

Brewers Publications. *The Classic Beer Style Series*, 1999. This series comprises fourteen books, each with a different author and each dealing with a particular beer style. Excellent detailed information.

Brewers Publications. *Microbrewers Resource Handbook and Directory*. A many-times-updated list of microbreweries, brewpubs, equipment manufacturers, consultants, brewing courses, journals, ingredient suppliers, etc. A bit light on Canadian information.

Briggs, D.E., J.S. Hough et al. *Malting and Brewing Science*, two volumes. Chapman and Hall, 1981. The standard textbook of British brewing practice from the 1970s to the present, and a must-have for any aspiring brewmaster.

Daniels, Ray. *Designing Great Beers*. Brewers Publications, 1996. Full of excellent information on formulating two dozen beer styles, how to calculate extract in wort, hop bitterness units, etc. Precise on ingredients and their effects. Another must for the small brewer.

De Clerck, J. *A Textbook of Brewing*, two volumes. Chapman and Hall, 1957. This classic text contains a wealth of information and drawings for the small brewer who must master the entire process of brewing.

Hind, H. Lloyd. *Brewing Science and Practise*, two volumes. Chapman and Hall, various editions 1937–56. The former standard text of British brewing, it's out of print but still available through used book dealers in the UK. Worth having. Brewing back then was very like craft brewing is today!

Jackson, Michael. *World Guide to Beer*. Prentice-Hall, 1977. The late, great beer writer's tribute to the beers of the world, including recognition of the North American craft beer revolution, then evolving. Lavishly illustrated.

Master Brewers Association of America. *The Practical Brewer*, 1981. An old standard dealing solely with large brewery operations.

Also: Brewers Publications, 1-888-822-6273, members. brewersassociation.org/store/. Lists many books of interest to small brewers. An offshoot of *The New Brewer* magazine.

Books on craft beer

Calagione, Sam. *Brewing Up a Business*. Wiley, 2011. Anyone thinking of starting a brewpub must read this book. Sam started with a tiny brewery and a belief in making "off-centred" ales in the first brewpub in Delaware. It took time and some hilarious setbacks, but he succeeded in making Dogfish Head a major craft brand in the US. His take on the business and marketplace aspect of craft beers is very perceptive.

Coutts, Ian. *Brew North*. Greystone Books, 2010. A witty account of "How Canadians made beer and beer made Canada," profusely illustrated. How the beer barons got as big as dinosaurs, leading to the emergence of "the New Guys." From John Molson to John Mitchell and Frank Appleton.

Hindy, Steve. *The Craft Beer Revolution*. Palgrave Macmillan, 2014. The co-founder of the Brooklyn Brewery gives an entrepreneur's look at how the business has evolved in the US.

Magee, Tony. *So You Want to Start a Brewery?* Chicago Review Press, 2012. The story of how Lagunitas Brewery survived and became a major name in California is replete with dramas, debacles and perseverance. An inspiring book for anyone venturing into the business.

Sneath, Allen Winn. *Brewed in Canada*. Dundurn Press, 2001. A complete, well-researched history of Canada's 350-year-old brewing industry, including the rise of real ales, brewpubs and microbreweries.

Stott, John C. *Beer Quest West*. TouchWood Editions, 2011. John Stott travels Alberta and BC to explore craft breweries and the people and stories behind them.

Wiebe, Joe. *Craft Beer Revolution*, 2nd ed. Douglas & McIntyre, 2015. The intrepid Joe Wiebe traverses BC to bring the reader a first-hand account of the booming craft beer business. His guide to the brewpubs and microbreweries is excellent; the second edition is updated.

About the Author

FRANK APPLETON HAS BEEN CONSULTANT BREWMASTER to twenty brewing operations, including consulting in brewery design, start-up and brewer training. In 2009, Appleton received the Lifetime Achievement Award for Leadership in Craft Brewing from CAMRA Chapter Victoria. He lives in Edgewood, BC.